THE JOURNEY OF MY LIFE FROM RWANDA

THE AMAZING TRUE STORY OF AN AFRICAN WOMAN'S LIFE

Chantal Batamuriza Mrimi

*To Ian & Fran,
With love & best
wishes,
from Chantal
Mrimi
19/2/15
x*

Bloomington, IN   authorHOUSE®   Milton Keynes, UK

AuthorHouse™
1663 Liberty Drive, Suite 200
Bloomington, IN 47403
www.authorhouse.com
Phone: 1-800-839-8640

AuthorHouse™ UK Ltd.
500 Avebury Boulevard
Central Milton Keynes, MK9 2BE
www.authorhouse.co.uk
Phone: 08001974150

First published by AuthorHouse 1/22/2007

ISBN: 978-1-4259-7312-4 (sc)

Printed in the United States of America
Bloomington, Indiana

This book is printed on acid-free paper.

This book is a work of non-fiction. Unless otherwise noted, the author
and the publisher make no explicit guarantees as to the accuracy of
the information contained in this book and in some cases, names of
people and places have been altered to protect their privacy.

"To every person whose innocent life has been prematurely ended by this world's on-going injustices; they include members of my family and fellow Rwandans, friends and fellow human beings. Adieu and rest in peace"

ACKNOWLEDGEMENTS

The stories in this book would have remained unpublished if it wasn't for the encouragement and support that I received from my psychiatric nurse Mrs May McArdle so thank you very much May for seeing a writer in me when I couldn't see one.

I will be eternally thankful to my church minister and his family for being there for me. They stood with me, cried with me and laughed with me. I can honestly say that life would have been a lot more difficult and painful without the help and support that I received and continue to receive from my minister and his family. I am also grateful to members of my church- InnerLeven Parish for their support, encouragement and prayers.

A day never passes by without me thinking how grateful and how thankful I am to my sponsor and her husband. The couple gave me a chance that transformed my life for better and forever.

Papa and mama, this book is for you - it is a testimony that if you love, support, encourage, guide and protect your children, then it means bringing up children who would achieve good things in their lives.

Thank you to all my family who have always been there for me. They include my brothers and sisters, all my aunties, uncles, cousins, sisters in law etc.

A big thank you to the father of my children who has been very kind, loving and caring since I met him that day in November 1997. His family has been the best family in law I could have wished for so thank you to all my family in law.

Thank you to all my friends in Britain and Rwanda who rallied to help, pray and support me when I most needed them - they include

Claire, Una, Michelle, Emma and the boys, Immaculee & Richard, my cousin Jussy, Margaret, Tecla, Michelle and Alistair, Pauline, Shany & Joseph, Karin and Joe, Juliet & Stuart, Aline, Helen, Blaise, Nabil and Lodha, Elsie & Nicholas, Mary & Method, Miriam & Jonathan, members of the Miracle Centre church, my colleagues Jackie, Ivy, Fiona, Naureen Alison, Murat, Norma, Amelia, Rhona, Jaspal, Mei, Ghada, Selma including some of our interpreters and many others. A big thank you to my manager Rina Ghosh for being not only a manager to me but a mentor and a close friend. Thanks must also go to my best friend Martin Alapi for being very encouraging and very kind.

A big thank you to my friend Min for all his help and support which include the lifts in the cold mornings, the lovely Chinese meals, the yoga classes.......Thank you.

Thanks to all who took part in the various prayers that were going on during the trials of my life.

A massive thank you to all my teachers in both primary and secondary schools and lecturers from HNC to BA in Administration Management for being very patient with me when learning the language and the course at the same time.

A massive thank you to Dr. Dickson, Dr. Michael and Stratheden hospital's nurses, doctors and other staff for providing me with the best health care that I needed.

Thank you to Gillian Stewart, Janice Murray and Yvonne for providing such a professional service to us.

Thank you to Dean Shah, my publishing advisor who has been very helpful and very patient as I struggled to come up with a title that made sense.

Thank you to Rimbleton Primary School's personnel including Mrs Mackinnon, Mrs Grubb and Mrs Hadden who were very helpful and very supportive to Nathan when he was going through hard times.

Thanks to Lorna, Gordon, Gillian and John for looking after Nathan and thanks to Heather and Pinewood Crèche for looking after Daniel.

Thanks to Joy's prayer cell of Vine church for having prayed and supported me.

Finally thank you to everyone who has touched my life in any way or form.

IN EXILE

"It's time to get ready for school" she shouted.

Mama was very good at shouting for us as we were always lost in local and traditional games with other children, not wanting to go home as there was nothing to go to; no food, no television, no radio, nothing!

"Alright mama, I'm coming in ten minutes" I replied.

"No ten minutes!" she shouted back.

She knew that ten minutes for me meant forever playing. Playing and having fun was the only way to put my suffering behind. The township where we lived was one of the most deprived parts of the city of Kisangani situated in the north of the Democratic Republic of Congo then known as Zaire. My parents were one of the few who put serious emphasis on the importance of their children's education.

"Come on! It's time to get ready so get out of there and come here now!"

"Ohhhhhhhhhh" I grumbled as I walked home towards the tiny bucket with little water to wash my face, hands and feet before putting on my school uniform. Unable to afford a watch or a clock, we used the size and position of our own shadow in the middle of sunshine to determine what the time was and amazingly we always got it right. If you couldn't see the shadow it meant noon.

One of the things I most hated about school was the fact that it was situated at about seven miles from where we lived and we had to walk the distance under the burning sun of midday to go there. The school catered for both primary and secondary school. The primary children occupied the school in the mornings from seven thirty until twelve thirty and the secondary children occupied the school between one o' clock till five thirty in the afternoon. When walking to school, the heat was sometimes unbearable because the equator crossed the city. I used to dream of growing up to become a doctor or professor in order to escape the natural cruelty of walking under the intense heat and drive a car or catch a bus to wherever I wanted. *"But how on earth will I ever achieve such a thing?"* I would wonder because looking at life around me, it was impossible to even imagine such a thing never mind hope that one would escape such extreme poverty. I was one of the many millions of children around the country to become victims of the Mobutu regime which saw many, many people lose their lives and everything they owned. People gradually sold their belongings in order to afford food, shelter, treatments and school fees for their children. Dishonesty and corruption became the most common ways to make money in this vast, naturally rich country. Civil servants like my father, who didn't believe in corruption and dishonesty, didn't have a life but worked non-stop in order to survive the hunger and chaos which lived with the poor on a daily basis. People were being exterminated slowly by this regime due to greed, corruption, mismanagement of resources, abuse of power and position, and partly due to peoples' intellectual blindness and lack of knowledge. The population were led to worship this dictator leader who had turned such a prosperous country into almost a desert where you had to pay bribes in order to access basic things such as drinking water. The psychological and physical damage left millions already dead ten to twenty years before their actual death - by this I mean people were helpless, hopeless and their motivation for life or success was non-existent. But life had to go on.

When I was born in 1975, life was fine. Not once did it cross my parents' minds that things would one day turn very bad. Back then, there was stability and public sector workers were paid well and money had value.

Having been through the then worst tribal conflict in Rwanda, my father had settled in Kisangani at the age of twenty two when he became a refugee in 1961. He was born in 1939 to a Tutsi family in Kirwa, a small town near Kigali, the capital city of Rwanda. Tutsis are believed to have originated from Ethiopia. Originally warrior-herders, the Tutsis entered Rwanda in the 14th or 15th century[1], settled and eventually ruled over the whole country. Tutsis retained their dominant position over the Hutus in Rwanda until 1961, when the monarch was overthrown. King Kigeli who was on a trip to Congo was told not to return to Rwanda. Like so many Rwandans, he has been in exile since.

When papa was five, his father, who had two wives, decided to emigrate to Uganda with his Belgian manager and his first wife. Papa and his mother remained in Rwanda staying with his maternal grandparents who were very rich. His years there were filled with good days as his grandpapa owned more than five hundreds cows. He remembers the sight of the huge field where cows fed and lay. The cows were in their hundreds and in different colours. Some were black, some were grey and some were white with black patches. His grandparents' house had lot of servants and shepherds.

In 1946, after the death of his grandparents and remarriage of his mother, papa was taken to live with the director of a school in Bugese, Ruhengeri, a district situated in north of Rwanda. The place where papa was sent to live was located 25km from where his mother lived.

Unlike the previous life at his grandparents where he was spoilt, life in Bugese with strangers was very hard. Papa was abused and used like a slave until one day in 1949 he decided that enough was enough and returned to his mother.

Since there was no school around his mother's place, papa was sent to an Anglican Missionary boarding school in Syhira where he excelled and became quite popular. He studied there until 1953 when he completed his primary school to attend secondary school at Shogwe Anglican Missionary's school. He successfully completed his secondary education in 1959 and began teaching at the missionary's primary school.

According to papa everyone lived together until the Belgian colonisers established themselves in the country. In order to cling on to power and colonisation, they supported and encouraged the majority Hutus to rise against the Tutsi leadership. They used division and created an ideology of ethnic hatred by turning to one tribe (Tutsis) and defining them as superior, clever, organised, rich etc and to the other (Hutus) as poor, inferior etc. This created an atmosphere of hatred which caused the loss of many hundreds of thousands of innocent lives over the last forty years.

When the fighting broke out in 1961, papa fled to Uganda because young men like him were being slaughtered first. Shortly before his exile to Uganda, he had impregnated Margarita, something quite unusual and unacceptable at that time. Although I have never had a detailed conversation with my father about his plans had he remained in Rwanda, I guess he would have married Margarita. However, papa somehow lost touch with Margarita due to war. In exile, he lost all hope of ever seeing her since they had not been in-touch for many years.

Unable to settle in Uganda, papa headed to Congo. He had nowhere to stay and nothing to eat when he arrived in Kisangani in 1961. The only thing he remembered to flee with was his smart black suit and a wooden case that had been given to him as presents by bwana (master) Stanley, an English missionary with the Anglican mission where he studied. After a few days of homelessness, he came up with an idea. He put on his smart suit and a few documents in his wooden case and off he went to the governor's home. At the entrance, he posed as an official from the Rwandese republic and was allowed in to see the governor. At the sitting room, he was first met by the governor's wife who kindly offered him a drink and conversed with him as he waited. As the conversation went on, fear and nervousness mounted within him for cheating his way in. He then decided to confide in her. As he explained his situation, the lady could only feel sympathy for what had happened to him and she promised to do what she could do in order to help him. She then went to see the governor before he came through and explained the whole situation to him. Luckily, he too felt sympathy and they both offered to accommodate him.

Papa was later employed by the governor as personal secretary, a job that he held until 1963 when Kisangani was attacked and captured by the rebels of Simba Murere. After four months of living in the forest like wild animals, the city was rescued by the government of Leopoldville (Kinshasa).

Papa was later that year admitted to the city's university where he studied for a management course. By now, he didn't know where his family was and had given up hope of seeing his mother and brother whom he had left in Rwanda. Towards the end of his course at the university, he met a Rwandan couple who had arrived from the city of Goma, eastern Congo. They told him that they knew the whereabouts of his mother and brother because they were together in Goma. What joy he had at the news! After securing the address, he immediately wrote to them. To his delight, they replied and soon after that they made arrangements to join him in Kisangani. Within a few months they were together. After weeks of celebrations, grand-mama and uncle Celestin settled well with uncle securing a local job. Soon after their arrival papa graduated and was offered a job at the same university.

On the other hand, my mother Collette was one of the youngest refugees to settle in the UNHCR camps located in Masisi, a small town near Goma where the United Nations and Zaire had made an agreement to settle thousands of refugees fleeing the war raging between Hutus and Tutsis. At age five, she didn't know much about the hard journey to exile.

Back then, the camps could only cater for primary education. Those who needed secondary education had to move to the nearest city of Goma. Parents had to either afford fees for boarding schools or find a relative in the city who was willing to accommodate their children whilst attending school otherwise it was impossible for them to attend secondary school. This situation however changed with time when the heavily forested place became a town with its own schools, hospitals etc.

When Collette completed her primary school in 1970, her parents sent her to attend secondary school in Goma where her cousin was staying with her family. It was agreed that Collette would help her look after the children and do some house work and in turn her cousin would pay for her school fees, provide accommodation and other expenses. Mama was lucky because not many girls had this chance. However, in 1973 her cousin was offered a scholarship at the University of Kisangani so the whole family including young Collette left for Kisangani. As her cousin became busier, it meant Collette had to concentrate on looking after the children and therefore could not continue with her schooling. A year later, she met my father and married in 1974. A dowry price[2] was sent via a local businessman to my grandparents because they could not afford to come to the wedding. They lived far away and needed a day's journey on road from Masisi to Goma and a flight from Goma to Kisangani, which was very expensive.

I came along in 1975, a joyful event to the newly married couple. They named me Chantal Batamuriza (my surname means don't make her cry). Soon after that my brother came along in 1977. My parents went on to have four more children making us six, until one day I learned from papa that there could be seven of us. I was about twelve when papa told me that I may have an older brother or sister somewhere in the world.

"Papa what are you talking about? I said naively thinking that he was joking.

"You know when the war broke out in Rwanda; I was in love with a girl?"

"Yes" I eagerly replied waiting for the story to follow.

"Well she was carrying my child when the war started and to this day I don't know what happened to them because I have never heard from the lady. So I don't know if she was killed in the war or is still alive. If she's still alive and had my child then it means you have a brother or a sister either in Rwanda or in exile somewhere in the world, just like us".

In exile! I was used to that word because everyday I was called refugee at school. A day never passed by without some children or even a teacher calling me a refugee or telling me to go back home to Rwanda. Rwandans and in particular Tutsis are easily recognisable because of their unique and distinct features so it made it easier for Congolese to pick on us. It also made it easier for the Hutu regime which was in power in Rwanda to discriminate against Tutsis. According to many of our extended family members and friends who lived in Rwanda, Tutsis didn't have equal access to basic rights such as education after secondary school. The regime also made it extremely hard for Tutsis to achieve anything such as being promoted at work or succeeding in business.

"Papa, if this child is alive somewhere, do you really think we are going to see him one day?" I asked in wonder.

"I hope so!" he replied looking rather sad.

I suppose he was missing his child even though he didn't know whether he/she existed. After learning that someone somewhere could be my brother or sister, thoughts would often run in my head trying to imagine their looks. I used to wonder *"what if I travel and meet a guy, I would have to really ensure that he wasn't my brother!"* Anyway, as time passed by we gave up hope of ever meeting this brother or sister of ours, but now and again we would talk about it.

KISANGANI, CONGO

The stronger the wind became, the tighter we had to hold on to the wooden pole that stood in the middle of the hut to support its iron roof. Strong wind made the hut we lived in swing from side to side.

"Mama, I'm scared!" I shouted.

"Don't give up! Keep holding!" she shouted back as the rain started to flow through the already weak roof.

Lightning and strong wind took part of the house which was already on the brink of falling even before the rain had started. Such was the type of house we lived in. After quite an aggressive forty minutes of rain and wind, they finally stopped and we managed to get out in the mud to assess the damage that the rain and wind had caused. Part of the wall was gone and the outside toilet that we used had fallen apart. Papa was at work that afternoon and didn't have a clue about what had happened to the small one bedroom rented hut that we all shared. We never had visitors inside the hut unless there was rain or wind because there was simply no room for people to sit. Six of us (children) shared the small two beds that were in what was supposed to be the sitting room. Our mattresses were made of dried grasses collected from rich people's gardens in the city. Papa and mama shared the only bedroom. There was no space to pass, never mind to store things so we stored clothes and households under the bed. Other things such as cooking utensils, plates, buckets were brought into the house at night time and placed in the middle of the house and were brought back outside first thing in the morning. Cooking took place outside in the court yard where there were three big stones placed in a triangular shape in order to support the pot. Underneath the pot was fire which produced a great deal of smoke. We had chronic red/crying eyes because of the constant smoke.

Just when we were walking around the house to see the damage, a neighbour came running "Oh my God, you will never believe what happened! A child playing football has been hit by the lightning and died instantly".

We had grown accustomed to such tragic news. Every day, a child in our neighbourhood had lost their little precious life either to malaria, measles, malnutrition or a natural cause such as lightning, drowning or other things. When the cause was unknown, people automatically blamed the death on witchcraft. Witchcraft was very common in the place where I was brought up. Everywhere you went, there were witch doctors, clairvoyants, sorcerers etc. So many stories would go around when someone died of unknown causes. Looking back I really feel I was misled by ignorant people. People could have died from many biological and natural causes but because there were no adequate health services to diagnose people's illnesses, it all fell under the witchcraft category.

One of our neighbours was a witch doctor. Every morning there was a ceremony taking place to call upon what is believed to be different spirits. The witch doctor would sacrifice a white chicken and would dress in white with white paint drawn on his face and hands. Animal skin and blood were part of the ceremony. Chanting and singing using local drums and other local musical instruments took place too. They worshipped these spirits and believed that if you did what they asked you (spirits' requests varied from a human life to a white chicken), then these spirits would in turn give you great wealth and heal you from any sickness. Adults and children were often believed to have been killed because the witch doctor said the spirits were asking to sacrifice either your child or a member of your family before it can grant your wish. People's wishes varied from healing of a disease to success in business. No wonder the African continent is going backwards rather than forward. People are stupidly led to believe that prosperity and wealth come from witchcraft rather than believing that you only get rich by working hard and using your brain not by sacrificing someone's life. Unfortunately some Africans, who are in business, still believe in human sacrifice for acquiring great wealth. We used to hear stories that after the death of the sacrificed relative, an appointment would be made for the client to meet with spirits and other creatures such as mar maid (known as mami wata) under the water and these meetings took place at midnight. What I know for sure is that often innocent lives were taken away because either they believed the person to be a witch or they sacrificed him/her. Our parents being from a totally different background kept us as far away as possible from these practices. However, living in the middle of it meant that we had to witness some of the sacrificing in particular the sacrificing of animals.

As we stood there shocked by the news of the child's death, we noticed that some of our neighbours' huts had also fallen apart. One of them was completely brought down. The family had to go and stay with their relatives for months before affording to build another little hut. As for ours, we used plastic sheeting to cover the broken wall until papa could afford to pay for a local builder to replace the collapsed wall. It took weeks before the wall was replaced. During this period we all had to share the only bedroom because we couldn't sleep in the damaged room. The small room was so crowded that the position you went to sleep in was the one that you woke up in, there was no room to turn or move. Unless you slept at the end of the room near the door, you couldn't even get up for toileting because it would mean getting everyone up in order to move and let you pass. The door was so small that most adults had to bend before entering the hut.

Things were made worst by the lack of payment of salaries. From the mid eighties onwards, the government often took up to ten months before paying civil servants and public sector workers' salaries. Day light robbery, bribes and corruption became people ways of making money to survive. Morale amongst soldiers and police known as gendarmes was so low that they often arrested innocent people for no reason. By 1990 most public workers including teachers, nurses, and police were always on strike to protest lack of payment by their bankrupt employers and government. University students were also on strike most of the time to protest lack of living allowances. It was very common to go to school and only learn half of what you were supposed to be learning because teachers couldn't be bothered to teach under the conditions. Often professionals such as university professors and doctors would walk to work without a decent pair of shoes. Cars and transport belonged to the minority who could afford it. Suffering became the norm and we literally lived like goats surviving on naturally grown herbs and all sorts of vegetation.

In 1993, my brother and sister aged five and two were so malnourished that we feared losing them. Their tummies had ballooned with other parts of the body so thin like a skeleton. They lost most of their hair and the remaining little hair had turned from its natural colour of black to brown/yellow. Fortunately there was a nutrition centre run by the catholic nuns where they were admitted on intensive nutritional programme which saved their lives. The only time we could afford to buy meat or fish was when papa got his salary back-paid. But the amount often found us in huge debt that the largest portion went to pay debtors. The remaining amount would make us happy for only two to three days.

NO PAINKILLER IN THE HOSPITAL WARD

In the eighties the quality of our lives started to deteriorate dramatically. By 1990 we could only live a day at a time. Public workers in particular were hit by the rapid national economic decline. It often took the government up to ten months to pay papa's salary. It was extremely hard to witness the needless deaths of close friends, young and old, due to lack of basic medicines in hospital wards. Death, poverty and suffering became part of our lives. I grew up thinking that was how life is meant to be because I didn't know any better until when I started to visit rich people house in the city. Malnutrition amongst young people became the norm. Luckily, charitable feeding centres became available to help those in great need. All sorts of eatable grass and vegetation became our main meal. Throughout my childhood, I could only own one pair of shoes and one proper dress at a time. There were times I didn't have shoes at all. At home, I was always wearing old, tired and often torn clothes. Once a year, mama took us to the big market in order to buy us second hand clothes which we only wore when going to the church or when visiting people. The day for shopping was always very exciting because it happened rarely. I had to wear sandals even when they had become too small. Most children couldn't attend school but we were very lucky to attend the university's school so the management didn't always sent us home for lack of school fees because they knew papa very well.

The most precious gift that we received from my parents was education. Without education and hard work, we would have remained in extreme poverty forever. However, it was very hard to learn under the conditions we had to endure. I often went to school with nothing in my stomach and the last few lessons sounded like music to my ears because I was either too weak to concentrate or too worried about if there was food at home for dinner. My favourite foods were rice and chicken but I could only eat these once or twice a year. My days were filled with dreams of how I was going to become rich one day and buy chicken and rice for dinner. I was fed up with eating cassava and its leaves everyday which were just boiled without oil or salt because we couldn't afford them. I hated it so much that once I went on for about four days without eating and on the fifth day I couldn't get out of bed. Mama managed to secure some maize flour and made me porridge which helped me regained some strength and energy.

It is almost impossible to describe the poverty that was around us. Basically, the quality of life was non-existent. The consequences of the poverty I experienced were not just the psychological trauma and low self esteem but countless deaths. I can't count the number of children including my best friends who had lost their precious lives as a result of the extreme poverty. I too nearly lost my life on many occasions due to lack of money for treatment. One of the serious cases was when I got struck by appendicitis. It was a beautiful afternoon; my brother and I were coming from fetching water at the nearby well. With the bucket on my head, I suddenly couldn't lift my right leg and couldn't move. My brother ran home for help and luckily papa was at home so he carried me to the University's hospital. At the hospital, the doctor examined me. It was my appendix which had become inflamed and needed to be removed as soon as possible otherwise it would erupt causing infection which could have been fatal.

"Can you operate on her now?" Papa asked.

"Yeah, we can operate on her as soon as you provide us with all operating materials" The doctor said. He went on to explain that there was nothing in the ward, not even a painkiller.

After finding out about what items he needed to buy at the pharmacy, papa nearly collapsed because to him the costs were staggering. There was no hope for me. I was lying in the ward's bed with unspeakable pain yet the whole hospital didn't have an aspirin or paracetamol to help me. Luckily there was a Rwandan doctor who owned a private hospital so papa decided to go and explain what had happened. He went to see him that evening and on hearing what had happened to me, he kindly accepted to admit me in his private hospital and conducted the surgery free of charge. Amazingly my family and I have lived to witness God providing for us when we least expected it. It was just miracle after miracle.

DREAMING

Although suffering and poverty around us was almost unimaginable, it did not stop me from dreaming of becoming rich one day. And my definition of rich at that time was to have a proper house with electricity and water in it; own a television and radio; eat meat and fish when I wanted to, own a car or afford the public transport etc. Because I had such an optimistic papa, he encouraged me to always think positive and think far. He worked in the admission office at the university and often new students from rich backgrounds would try to bribe him so that he would admit them at the university. Rather than accepting their bribes, he would ask them for a favour. He wanted them to allow me to visit their houses so that my horizons would not be limited to the extreme poverty that we lived in but rather if I could see with my very own eyes the beauty of owning good things then it would perhaps motivate me to succeed. And it worked because once I started to visit rich people's houses, all I could think of was how I was going to make it to where these rich people were. I was also lucky to have a wealthy godmother. She was a lady from Rwanda who was in charge of a well known hotel. Because she had no family, she often had me stay with her at the weekends. During my stay, I would meet other wealthy people and chat with them. Although I was young, people were often amazed at the determination I had to succeed. Psychologically, I found it very hard to accept the massive gap that existed between rich people I visited and the extremely poor people around me - but there was nothing I could do about it. However I found it very helpful to be around rich people's homes because it created a confidence in me and it also broadened my mind. Not many children where I lived had the same chance as me and the fact that they could only see these nice huge houses from a distance often made them feel they didn't belong to this kind of rich middle class society, whereas for me I had the chance to walk through the heavy iron gates and sit in these huge, beautiful sitting rooms. The short interaction and contact that I had with rich people made me feel welcome and drove me to believe that after all they too were humans like us. The gap and fear of rich people that I had in me disappeared slowly and I found myself learning a lot from their success be it business or career. It was during my stay at my godmother's that I met one of the most powerful men in the local government. He was the first adviser to the region's governor. One day, he said to me,

"I find you and your questions interesting. Here's my business card, if you need anything, just ask". He later became one of the people who played a role in the success of my life.

GENOCIDE IN RWANDA AND THE VICTORY OF THE RWANDAN PATRIOTIC FRONT (RPF)

As proud Rwandans, my parents kept a close link with Rwanda through mixing with the Rwandan community and through news and letters from extended family, who had remained in Rwanda. They also insisted that we learned the language and culture, which we did to a certain extent. Like many other Rwandans around the world, their biggest wish was to return to Rwanda one day. Papa in particular loved Rwanda very much; he was very patriotic and missed his beloved country very much. A day never passed by without him telling us a story about Rwanda. It was therefore with excitement that he heard of the first attacks by the Tutsi rebels known as Rwandan Patriotic Front (RPF) in 1990. His hope was that the rebels would win the battle and the victory would allow us to go back to Rwanda freely, without fear of persecution by the Hutu regime. Like many other Rwandan communities around the world, ours became very much involved. Special meetings and fundraising events were organised. Young people left to join the rebels who were based in Uganda. This was our only hope to return to our beloved land of origin and escape from the cruelty of poverty and the stigma that was attached to refugees. We supported the rebels by sending funds raised, messages of encouragement, prayers etc. Adults' ears were hooked on the radio (BBC world news and Voice of America) because they gave a fair view of what was happening in Rwanda. Papa had a small radio that he listened to almost twenty four hours a day, waiting to hear anything to do with the RPF.

As negotiations between the government of Rwanda and the RPF went on, we felt closer to returning to Rwanda. Even though I wanted to escape from Kisangani, there was a sense of fear and uncertainty because we had never been to Rwanda before. And yet we felt it would be the right thing to do, to move to Rwanda immediately if and when the RPF was to take over the country. However, as years passed by, we felt the negotiations were leading to nothing tangible. All we could do was to wait and pray that our hopes and dreams would come true.

On the evening of 6th April 1994, papa couldn't believe his ears when he heard on the radio that president Habyarimana of the then Rwandan government had been killed in a plane crash. That evening, we were outside gathered as usual for the night time story by mama. Papa had a chair (chaise longue) which was known to belong to only him so we were used to sitting or lying on the mat with mama in the middle of us telling us stories and tales. Papa always had his portable radio with him. In the middle of the storytelling, we heard him shout saying:

"My God, this is incredible! This is unbelievable! The person proven to be the obstacle to our returning to Rwanda has died, thank God! At last we are going to go back without any problem."

We joined him in celebration and the storytelling turned into a conversation surrounding the president's death.

Papa couldn't wait to see his fellow Rwandans the next day in order to celebrate. It never once crossed his mind or ours that something dreadful was going to follow. As he spent all night listening to the BBC radio, he started to realise what was going to happen to Tutsis living in Rwanda because as time went by, tensions rose in Rwanda.

The following morning saw a number of road blocks in place and the massacre of so many innocent people began. Celebrations turned into mourning; joy and hope that had once filled Rwandans at the death of the president turned into sorrow, despair and hopelessness. We could only watch, wait and hope that our people would be rescued and delivered before it was too late. How wrong we were! The small number of blue berets (United Nations' peace keepers) that were already in the country started to evacuate foreigners, and then they themselves left. The world which had vowed never to allow genocide to happen again was watching and yet it failed to intervene and stop the barbaric slaughter of hundreds of thousands. It was as if the world had stood still. All we could do was to pray for the peace of Rwanda. The atmosphere was very sad, sombre and hopeless. Young people in our Rwandan community felt moved and most of them left to join the rebels in order to try and save their fellow Rwandans' lives because no one else was doing it. If the 100 days that followed were the worst in my entire life, what about those who were directly affected? I could only imagine the torment, torture, despair, fear and pain that they were going through. My beloved family (aunties, uncles and cousins) in Rwanda that I often dreamed of seeing, were they still alive? I wondered.

"How could Rwandans kill so many other Rwandans?" I asked papa.

"This tribal conflict is a long and old one" he said. It will take a long time to reconcile the two tribes after what's happening now".

The more people got killed in Rwanda, the more hatred and abuse we received from the Congolese. They called us cold hearted killers who would kill them one day and therefore were no longer welcome to stay in their country. School became almost impossible to attend because of bullying and abuse. Often the abuse was so physical that people were treated for serious injuries.

In July, after so many tears and much hopelessness, news that the RPF had taken control of the whole country was most welcomed. We were very relieved to hear that the government, which had systematically planned and carried out these killings, was ousted. Although we were all mourning for our people and fearing for our lives as insecurity of Rwandans in Congo increased, we couldn't resist celebrating. We dedicated the victory of the RPF to our beloved Rwandans who had lost their lives because of their identity. Kagame who is currently the president of Rwanda and his team immediately began the task of rebuilding the country that was shattered by one of the worst genocides in modern history. He invited and welcomed every Rwandan across the globe to come and be part of the rebuilding programme. After the loss of many skilled and working age people, Rwanda was in great need of experienced staff like papa. He had been working for the university for over twenty years. For us as a family, this was the opportunity for us to start again. The fact that we had lost so many people, Rwanda needed us and we needed it too - after all it was our land of origin and after more than thirty years in exile, who wouldn't be glad to go back to his country.

About eighty percent of the Rwandan community in Kisangani were well off and could afford to move to Rwanda. The remaining twenty percent, like us, didn't have a clue how we were going to afford plane tickets to go back and yet we were the ones at more risk because we stayed in poor, rundown areas where violence and abuse was very common and occurred on a daily basis.

LIFT ON THE CARGO PLANE

Within a month of the RPF victory, half of the Rwandan community had gone back to Rwanda. We envied their position because we couldn't afford to leave. Every evening, we met as a family to discuss ways of going to Rwanda but each solution we came up with would fail practically. One day in September, an idea came to my head as I lay in my bed. Afraid that it would fail like the other ideas we had, I decided to go ahead without telling my family so that if it failed they would not be disappointed because they did not know about it. On my way to my godmother, I decided to pay a visit to the director of Zaire Airlines. At the office, I was met by the receptionist/secretary to whom I explained the whole situation. However, she decided not to let me see the director because she thought there was nothing he could have done. Disappointed but equally determined, I left the office with another plan. I knew that if I could meet this guy and cry out my eyes to him, hopefully he would sympathise and authorise to fly us free of charge. It was a dream worth trying. I decided to go to his residence which was located in a very posh and secure area. My grandmother had taught me different traditional handcrafts which I used to sell.

The objects that grand-mama and I made were quite unusual because they were Rwandan handcrafts so I often got most people interested in buying them. I used to sell them in offices, homes and at the market. I took some of the baskets and ornamental objects that grand-mama and I had made and went to the director's home. At the gates I explained to the keeper that I wanted to sell these objects to the lady of the house. He took them and left me at the gates in order to ask Madame Gilbert if she wanted to buy them. Moments later the gate keeper came and told me that she was interested in the objects and wanted to talk to me. *"Hallelujah!"* I thought as I said a quick prayer in my heart. Madame Gilbert, a beautiful, mixed race, middle aged woman was waiting for me at their beautiful balcony. She greeted me and started chatting about the handcrafts and how I made them. She bought some of them and asked me to return with some more. After handing me the cash, I gathered my thoughts together and nervously said:

"Madame, I have something to ask you. Now that I am here, you are my only hope."

"What can I do for you?" she asked.

"You see I come from a Rwandan family. We are very poor and as you are probably aware, Rwandans are increasingly becoming the target of a hate campaign since the genocide started. We are increasingly feeling very insecure in this country as abuse and violence against us increase on a daily basis. After the victory of the Rwandan Patriotic Front, we now have the chance to return to Rwanda without fear of persecution but we haven't got any money to buy the flight tickets. So please help us because we have no future nor hope in this place. I am begging you to have mercy and do all that you can to help us. Even if you could secure us places aboard a commercial cargo, we are ready to go."

"Child, you know this is a very hard and an almost impossible request that you are making?" she said.

"Yes Madame! I do" I replied

"Besides I don't see how I can practically help you and your family to fly out of this country."

At this I said, "I was thinking maybe you could please pass my request to Mr Gilbert in order to see if he could authorise us to go free of charge. I went to see him in his office in order to personally ask him but the secretary wouldn't let me see him and that's why I am here instead, so please at least speak to him."

After quite a long conversation about how I thought moving to Rwanda was going to help us, she at last agreed to have a word with her husband. She asked me to return a week later.

At home they could not believe me when I told them about my little adventure at Mr Gilbert's house. From that evening onwards, we prayed that God would perform a miracle. It was something that I had never heard of, a free flight on the plane, but I believed in miracles. We had our doubts as to how this request was going to be successful but we trusted God to work on Mr and Mrs Gilbert.

When the day arrived, I was nervous, scared and hopeful. Even though I was convinced that this would not work, deep down my heart I hoped for a miracle. My parents blessed me and prayed with me that morning before I left. At the gates, I nervously waited as the keeper confirmed with Madame Gilbert about my appointment. We met again at the beautiful balcony. After the usual greetings she started to explain how Mr Gilbert would have loved to help but it was impossible to fly the whole family because this was a business and could not afford to do so. However, Mr Gilbert could help take one person on one of their cargo planes leaving the following week and that was all they could afford to do.

"Thank you very much, I said. It is very kind of you to have tried. I am very grateful and please keep the place for us. I will speak to my family and decide who should go first. I will give you the details of the passenger as soon as possible".

As I rushed home to tell them the news, all I could think of was who was going to go first. It had to be papa or mama. We (the children) were too young for one of us to be sent to a new country without any family. Once at home I found mama waiting and the first question

"How did it go?"

"Not as well as I had hoped but they have agreed to let one person travel free of charge" I said.

"That's wonderful!" mama said. "Your papa could go first. Hopefully he would get a job and pay for us to join him."

When papa came home, he was equally pleased to hear that one of us was given a chance to go. That night, the entire family agreed that it was best for my father to go. After thanking me for my efforts, we began to prepare for his journey.

With not a penny to spend, we could not imagine his life in Rwanda without money, so the following day I went to my godmother and told her what had happened.

"We need some help for papa's spending money, please help us with anything that you can," I said.

"I will see what I can do," she replied.

After spending a day with her, it was time to leave and when she said goodbye she handed me some folded money. On my way home, I was delighted to discover that she had handed me $100. It was a lot of money to us, so much that it could have fed us on basic foods for four months. For my family it was another miracle.

"You are very blessed, Chantal. You have just achieved something that could change our lives as a family. Come here, my princess," papa said, as he put his arms round me embracing me with a fatherly hug of gratefulness. Even though I'd always been driven to help my family by selling the crafts that grand-mama and I made, this event made my family think I was extra special.

On 12th September 1994 we had papa's small suitcase packed and took him to the airport. It was very emotional. We had our fears; we didn't know if we would see each other again. But it was an opportunity that could change our lives. As papa hugged me before boarding the cargo plane, he whispered in my ears,

"Look after your mama and your brothers and sisters. I leave you in charge and I know you are more than capable".

"Yes papa, I promise to look after them," I said with tears rolling down my cheeks. We waved goodbye.

Papa had left us $50 and a vegetable field. The field belonged to the university where papa worked. The university had borrowed him the field in order to grow crops for our survival. We spent most evenings and weekends cultivating the land. Work included cutting the long grass and burning it. Once the field was cleared of long grass, we had to cultivate the land to prepare it for planting. During the planting seasons my brother and I were wakened early in the morning to go and do some work before school time. Everyday, before going to school, we had to go to the field to ensure that there were no weeds or bad grass to spoil the growing of vegetables. This was followed by the harvest time which I most enjoyed. I loved the harvest as it meant getting the results of our hard work. Because the land was very fertile, vegetables and fruits looked beautiful and were delicious. Although I hated working on the field, I enjoyed the teamwork. There were usually four or five of us in our field. The next field would have another three or four people. After the hard work we would all gather under the shadow of a tree to take refreshments and snacks. However we had to be very careful because there were always poisonous snakes everywhere. We had to always carry a special black stone which is supposed to suck poison from your blood stream if you are bitten by a poisonous snake. The field produced enough maize, sweet potatoes, cassava, aubergines, tomato etc for our use and for sale. Proceeds from the sale of vegetables were so little that we could only buy salt, sugar, soap etc.

The lack of a reliable post service and other communication means meant that we had to wait for someone going to or coming from Rwanda to hear from papa or for him to hear from us. Luckily there were people going back and forward regularly. So it was with excitement that we received his first letter six weeks after his departure. The letter was very long and very interesting. In it, he had explained how it felt to arrive in his homeland after thirty three years in exile. As soon as he crossed the border, he lay down and kissed the ground. Soldiers guarding the borders were used to these scenes and therefore gave people their time. He thought that he was dreaming but it was real. He hugged the soldiers as they checked his identification. Since he had nowhere to stay and it was getting dark, they offered him a place for the night. The following morning, he was on his way to Kigali, the capital city. After a three hour journey, he arrived in Kigali. Unable to contain his joy and excitement, tears started to roll down his cheeks. Even though throughout his life, he had hoped to see his beloved country one day, he could not believe he was there in the middle of Kigali. However there was only one problem; the same problem he faced when he left the country in 1961 was facing him again on his return to the country; he had nowhere to stay and did not have enough money to pay for accommodation. He didn't know anybody. He did not even know where the Rwandans from Kisangani stayed. After changing his $50 in local money, he sat at the bus station's café planning his next move. Next to him was a young, tall, dark man.

Papa approached him and started talking to him. As the conversation went on, he asked him for a place to stay until he located people he knew. Luckily the gentleman said yes. Papa went to stay with him and his family for the next couple of months. He became part of his family. It was a relief to hear that he had somewhere to stay. The bad news was that he was still hunting for a job. Without a job, our chance of getting our tickets was non-existent. Violence and abuse against us became a daily occurrence. Death treats were very common. Rwandans across the country were being attacked and intimidated. We had to be home by five o' clock in the afternoon. None of us was allowed to leave the house by themselves. Mama feared most for me and my younger sisters because a few girls had been raped so she kept a close eye on us.

NO HOPE

In November a second letter from papa arrived. He had moved to stay with one of his relatives in the massive house that they had taken after the war. Shortly after the war, people helped themselves to properties that had been abandoned by their owners. It was very common to see an empty house and stay in it without anybody's permission. But years later, owners claimed back their properties. Up to now, he still had not got a job. However he had met a lot of his relatives whom he had not seen for over thirty years. Many of his relatives had been killed in the war and had left orphans. These orphans looked to him for help plus his family was waiting for tickets; so finding a job was compulsory but it was not easy. In his letter, papa expressed his fears of not seeing us for years because not only did he not have a job but even if he got one, the salaries were not that great. The average salary for a public worker was about US$120 per month. A ticket for one person would cost about US$270. With such a job, it would take him years to save enough money for us to join him. After reading the letter, we felt the same too. We felt that it would be years before we could join him.

Because we could no longer dwell on the fact that papa would get a job and take us to Rwanda, I became more determined to get us out of this situation. After days and nights of thinking how we were going to go to Rwanda, I came up with a plan similar to the one I had used earlier to get papa to Rwanda. This time I was going to see the first adviser to the region's governor whom I had met before. One night, I discussed the plan with mama and she gave me her blessing but warned me to be very careful because young women like me were often used by big men like the one I was going to see for sex purposes.

In Africa and in particular in Congo, it was very common for big bosses to lure young girls from poor backgrounds into sexual activities in exchange for services or small amounts of money. I remember once when I went to sell my crafts at the mayor's office. My intention was to sell them to the office staff but somehow the objects ended up on the mayor's desk. I was called to see him. I'd never been to such a magnificent office before. It was a huge, well decorated room which smelt nice with the air conditioner on. Behind the immaculate big desk was a big fat man. I was shaking with fear because of his title but was equally happy that I was now going to cash in a lot of money. I charged him almost double the usual price because I knew how rich this guy was. On my second trip to his office, because he'd asked me to return with more objects, I was shocked and petrified to hear his sexual language. He wanted to meet with me in a posh hotel and was prepared to pay me a fortune for it. Luckily, I always carried the warnings about any sexual activity by my parents with me so I declined his offer and was relieved to be out of his sight. Not only had papa warned me about early pregnancy when you sleep with boys but he'd made it clear that any sexual activity at that immature age meant a death sentence by HIV Aids. I was therefore wary to engage in any kind of sexual activity before the legal and mature age regardless of what it paid or who it was with.

After getting mama's permission, the following day I went to the governor's office. After so many checks the guards finally allowed me to enter the office. At the reception of the first advisor's office, I was met by the secretary who after taking her time, went and confirmed with Mr Ngando that I was there to see him.

"Come in," the smartly dressed, middle aged man said as he met me at the door.

"Nice to see you again" he said as he showed me where to sit in his immaculate office.

"Praise God, he remembers me" I whispered to myself.

"Good to see you too, sir" I nervously replied.

"How is Madame Pauline?" he asked, referring to my godmother who ran the hotel where we had first met.

"She is fine. I saw her last weekend. How are you sir? I wasn't sure you would remember me" I nervously but confidently said.

"Of course I do remember you, who can forget a beautiful girl like you".

I was very flattered by this comment.

"Would you like something to drink?" he asked as he walked towards the fridge where refreshments were kept.

"Yes sir, some juice please".

The more he spoke to me, the more I panicked because I started to clearly see the motives behind his flattery and sweet language. It is as if meat had brought itself to the table and by this I mean a young girl bringing herself to the office of a big boss like him.

Eventually, the words I was waiting for came.

"What can I do for you, my dear Chantal?"

"Sir, I am here because I need help and I would like to talk to the governor. The only way to get to him was to see you so that you can grant me an audience with him".

"What is it that you want him to help you with?" he curiously asked.

"Well! I will tell you the whole story, maybe you can help me" I said.

"I am the eldest of six children; we are currently living with my grand-mama who is very poor. My mother is currently in Goma and hasn't been well for a while - she is unable to provide for us. It has been extremely difficult to provide and look after my young sisters & brothers and grand-mama. Also, since the Rwandan genocide it has been extremely hard for us, as Rwandans are now the target of a hate campaign. We have been threatened on many occasions and I am always scared that something horrible is going to happen. We would like to join mama in Goma but we can't afford it so I am here to beg you or the governor for help. Perhaps you could speak to one of the airline companies in order to secure us places aboard a cargo plane free of charge. If we remain here, we have no chance of surviving so please help us. We are in a very desperate situation".

He took a deep breath before calmly replying that, the request was something that he'd never been asked for in the past and that it was very hard to help. After quite a long conversation in which I begged him to try and help, he finally agreed to try and do something about it. However the look on his face as he said this expressed that he was expecting something back which I interpreted as asking me to go out with him. As I left, he held my hand and looked me in my eyes and said,

"I would do all that I can to help a young and beautiful girl like you." I was so relieved to leave his office because I began to feel as if I had set myself a trap. He asked me to come and see him a week later.

At home, I told mama everything except the fear that I had regarding this man's expectations. We started to pray for another miracle to happen. Even if it meant taking another person, it would reduce the costs. Meantime I tried to seek help from Rwandan rich people but none of them could help because they too had been preparing and spending on their moving to Rwanda. Everybody was busy leaving. We felt hopeless and helpless, yet the dream of reaching Rwanda stayed there all the time.

ANOTHER MIRACLE

A week later I went to my appointment. Before leaving, mama wanted me to take my brother Emmanuel.

"Mama I will be alright" I said as I declined her offer to take my brother.

At the gates, the guards recognised me and let me in, this time without any hassle. The secretary was much kinder perhaps because she saw how long I had spent with her boss the last time. After a few minutes, I entered Mr Kunda's office.

"Hello Chantal, how are you?"

This time I was surprised to see that he had the courage of kissing me on my cheeks, something that he had never done before. Feeling quite embarrassed I said

"Fine, Mr Kunda."

"Well I have some good news and bad news", he continued.

"The good news is that I have found an airline company that is willing to help you and the bad news is that they are willing to take only three people aboard their cargo. They can't afford to take more than three, I am afraid. However I'm still waiting to hear from other companies. I suggest that you send three of your brothers and sisters - hopefully other companies will get back to me and we will see if you and the remaining relatives can then join the family."

"It's wonderful" I gratefully said feeling very excited at the fact that my plan had not completely failed.

"The plane will leave in ten days. I need you to give me the details of those going as soon as possible."

"Yes sir, I shall bring the details tomorrow after I discuss with my family who is to go."

At home they were eagerly waiting for the news and as soon as they saw me, they all came running towards me asking me, "How did it go?"

"Mama, a company has accepted to take three of us." I don't know where she got the strength to lift me up as joy and hope filled her eyes.

"God is good" she cried. "All we have to do now is decide who will go first."

"Mama you should go with the two younger children because Mr Kunda knows me and is trying his best to find us another company to bring us," I suggested

"No way am I going to leave you in this country on your own," mama said. You and two of your sisters must go and God will find us ways of joining you."

"But mama, the guy doesn't know you plus I told him you are in Goma, so I don't think he would want to follow up the situation if it isn't I who is here to ensure that he does."

"My child, I understand perfectly what you are saying but I will never forgive myself if anything happened to you. You know how people around here are getting increasingly hostile. They could easily take advantage of our absence to rape you or even kill you, so it's my wish that you, Annie and Marie go instead."

After an intense family debate, we decided that it was best for me and my two young sisters to go. My brother Emmanuel, who was seventeen at the time, Louis who was six and Charlotte who was two, would stay with mama.

As promised, the next day I went to provide Mr Kunda with our details. He was surprised to see that I was one of the passengers.

"Grand-mama has insisted that I go" I said.

"Well, if that's what you've decided, it's fine with me."

After sincerely thanking this good man, I left. Realising that I had just confirmed our tickets to Goma en route to Rwanda I suddenly felt excited and scared at the same time. Excited that I was going to a new country where things would hopefully be far better than where I was, fear that I was going to travel on my own and in charge of my two sisters, Annie who was twelve and Marie who was nine. With the help of a few friends, we managed to collect about US$60 for our spending money. Mama drew an action plan for me because she was very nervous about sending us to Rwanda.

"When you land in Goma you must take a taxi to Okapi," mama said. Once at Okapi, ask for Mr Tubane."

Mr Tubane was a family friend who had moved to live in Goma and was working for Okapi - a company that produced cigarettes.

"He will help you to cross the border and will recommend you to his friends in Gisenyi (Rwanda) who will then help you on how to get to Kigali where your papa is."

In his last letter, papa had explained how Mr Munka (one of the Rwandans who had lived in Kisangani) had opened a shop near Kigali's main bus station. The shop became a meeting point for people from Kisangani and Mr Munka often knew the whereabouts of most Rwandans who had lived in Kisangani, now living in Kigali. Mama gave me the name of the shop and told me to go straight to the shop once we arrived in Kigali.

After quite a long and what seemed to be an everlasting training from mama on how to be careful and take care, the day of flying came.

Since there was no time and no means to communicate with papa, he did not have a clue that we were on our way to Kigali.

KIGALI, RWANDA

Excited, happy, scared and sad we left for the airport on 23rd December 1994. The flight was at eleven in the morning. After a very emotional farewell, we took our place in the huge cargo plane packed with building materials going to Goma. There were a few chairs at the back of the aircraft but they did not have seatbelts - not that I knew what seatbelts were. The vast plane looked like a warehouse inside. The crew were dressed in overalls and were very chatty, friendly and really nice. As I looked around me, I feared for our lives because I was not convinced how a huge, heavy thing like the plane we were in could leave the ground and fly. As the engine started to make a noise, so my heartbeat rose. I have never been so scared in my life. As the plane started to move, the three of us held hands. Before we knew it, the plane was speeding and soon after that we were in the air. As I looked from the window with one eye closed and another opened, I couldn't believe what was happening to us. Thoughts started to run through my mind including: *"Adieu Kisangani the city of my birth, the city of my upbringing. Although I knew much misery and poverty here, I shall miss you terribly because I love you. Don't keep mama, sister and brothers forever with you. Send them soon to be with us as we start a brand new life in a brand new country."*

I couldn't help but cry. My sisters were too young to understand my feelings. I was old enough to feel nostalgia and fear.

After an hour and forty minutes, we landed at Goma airport. One of the crew who was familiar with the area helped us get a taxi to Okapi where we met a much surprised Mr Tubane. He immediately took the afternoon off in order to help us. After we had a lovely meal with his family, he took us to the border at around five thirty in the afternoon. One of the things that amazed me, were the hills and mountains of Goma and Rwanda. Never in my life had I seen a hill, never mind a mountain. I studied them in Geography and saw them in photos and films so seeing them face to face was fascinating. Kisangani was a very plain place. You could drive hundreds of miles without seeing a hill. Not even many valleys existed in Kisangani. Geographically speaking, it was quite boring.

As soon as we arrived at the Rwandan border, I could tell we were in a very different country. Even though it's my country of origin, it felt very foreign. The people looked very different from the Congolese that I was used to seeing everyday. The language spoken was Kinyarwanda whereas in Congo, at home we spoke in Lingala or Swahili and spoke French at school; you were punished if you were caught speaking in any other language. Mr Tubane telephoned his friends who came to collect us from the border. The soldiers at the border were very kind and told us to learn Kinyarwanda. We stayed with our hosts for a night and the following morning, which was the morning of Christmas Eve, they put us on a bus to Kigali. On the way, I enjoyed looking at the hills and mountains. The roads were not straight; it was like driving on a zigzag road. After climbing a big mountain, I would look from the bus window only to see the road we had been driving on far below us. It was a very scary experience. I was very amazed to see how people managed to construct roads around these huge mountains. As we approached Kigali, I felt closer to seeing papa. I was full of joy too because I felt closer to realising my big hope that we had escaped from horrible poverty. However my joy was cut short by the smell and look of the city. Buildings were destroyed and the city looked chaotic.

"Oh no, this is horrible. I don't like this," I thought to myself.

It really felt like we had made the wrong move. I couldn't imagine me being happy in this war looking zone. Although we understood the language, we could not speak it and it frustrated me to see that nobody was speaking in the languages that I knew. We arrived in Kigali at around one o clock in the afternoon. After much effort of seeking directions to the shop, we finally entered Mr Munka's shop. Mr Munka was shocked to see us. After greeting us, he told us how papa had been to see him the day before.

"He was here yesterday and he's just got a job with the Ministry of Education" he said. "The ministry of education is in Kacyiru."

He advised us to leave our luggage with him and go to see papa first. Luckily there was a bus stop in front of the building where papa worked. After getting us on the right bus, we went to meet papa. We were so excited. I was very relieved to hear that papa had got a job because it meant he had some income to support us. At the bus stop, the driver kindly showed us the right building. It was about two thirty when we arrived at the main reception. This was like the event of my lifetime - meeting papa after such uncertainty of never seeing him again for a very long time. The receptionist told us to go to his office which was on the third floor. With my sisters by my side, I excitedly and nervously knocked on the door. I was shaking.

A female voice said come in. *"It's not papa" I thought.*

"Hello" I said as I opened the door.

"We are looking for Mr Charles." I continued.

"He is not back from his lunch yet but should be back soon" she replied.

After we explained who we were, she asked us to wait for him at the main reception which was downstairs. As we came down the stairs, I could hear papa's voice. We met halfway down the staircase.

"Hello papa" I said almost not believing what I was seeing.

He nearly ran away thinking that he'd seen our ghosts.

"This can't possibly be true" he said as he opened his eyes wide as if to confirm that it was really us and not our ghosts.

The staircase became too small for the huge and emotional hug between the four of us. It was my first time to see papa in tears. All he kept saying was "ce n'est pas possible" which means it's not possible.

"But how did you manage to come? He curiously asked looking shocked and amazed

"This is incredible; it's a miracle to see you! Where is the rest of the family? Are they okay?"

"Yes papa they are fine - our coming is a long story" I said.

After spending a few minutes on the staircase, he took us to his office where he introduced us to everybody and then took the rest of the day off. We went to a nearby restaurant to catch up. We were given so much food. I was very happy to eat chicken and chips after a very long time. Papa spoilt us very much and listened in amazement as we told him how we had managed to come. We then left to collect our luggage and went home to his two bedroom rented house in Kacyiru. It took him days to believe that we were really in Rwanda. It was the best Christmas present for all of us even though we were missing mama and the other children so much. At least papa didn't have to spend Christmas on his own.

On Christmas day, we went to the local pub where we met many people who had come to Rwanda from around the world. It felt very strange, emotional and weird to be in Rwanda. We were struggling to speak Kinyarwanda even though we understood most words. The city was still recovering from the genocide which had taken place only a few moths before our arrival. Buildings were destroyed and the loss of so many people during the war was beyond anyone's imagination. Survivors of the genocide were still coming to terms with what had happened to them. Like many Rwandan families, we as a family were struggling to come to terms with the loss of many members of my family. Most of papa's family were in Rwanda so many of them became victims of the genocide. When we visited papa's village, we only found a handful of people and the remaining members of the family were lying dead in mass graves not so far from the field. If it is the murder of one person, then you feel the pain and anger but when your family is murdered in dozens then nothing can describe how you feel. I was numb, frozen and in denial for a long time. I didn't want to accept and believe that the genocide took place in my country. For a long time I tried to think of it as a bad and horrible nightmare which would go away the next day but sadly it wasn't a nightmare. After realising that the genocide was true, I started to hate Hutus. I felt very angry and bitter. I tried to overcome my anger and bitterness for Hutus - however I couldn't help it but feel physically sick whenever I came across them. What made the healing process even longer was the fact that we had to live with Hutus who were suspected of being involved in the genocide. Survivors of the genocide would often show us these cold hearted killers walking and living freely. We often had orphans and survivors of the genocide stay with us - the atmosphere was always sombre and sad. For many months and indeed for many years, it felt like climbing a huge mountain. It is only after I became a born again Christian that I started to learn how to forgive those who killed others in the genocide. I also learned to take into consideration the reasons behind the horrendous killings. I learned to blame not only one side but the history of our country which has long divided our tribes instead of uniting them. I learned to blame the leaders and national/local media who not only orchestrated these mass murders but brainwashed ignorant and illiterate people by turning them into militia and cold hearted killers.

The months of April to July are very hard for Rwandans because that's when the genocide took place. These months are a dark period in my calendar but I try my best to move on and focus on how we Rwandans across the globe should help our country to overcome such a hate and tribalism in order to avoid such a horrible disaster from happening again.

Upon our arrival in the country, things were still very difficult for people and for the government of Rwanda. For instance, hospitals were filled with injured people and the only psychiatric hospital that served the whole country was packed beyond limit. Prisons were overcrowded. It wasn't unusual to stumble over dead bodies which had been buried in mass graves - everywhere you went there were mass graves. The river which provided household water was recently full of bodies so we had to constantly boil water for cooking and drinking. Socially, Kigali had become a multicultural city over night. Many of the Rwandans who had been in exile in many different parts of the world moved to Kigali. Most of them were from neighbouring DR Congo, Burundi, Uganda, Kenya and Tanzania. The society was divided into two categories; the Anglophone who were from English speaking countries such as Uganda, Kenya, Tanzania etc and the Francophone who were from French speaking countries such as Rwanda, Burundi, and Congo. The presence of heavy military police was everywhere. The challenges before us were great. We had to learn the language and we had to accept other people's culture which was very different from ours. For example people from Uganda are reserved whereas people from Congo are very open and outgoing. Some of our next door neighbours were from Rwanda and Uganda and others were from Burundi and Congo. At this point, the language became one of my biggest challenges as

I spoke very little Kinyarwanda. I remember my first experience of shopping in the market where most people spoke in Kinyarwanda. I wanted to buy small aubergines which are known as nyanya in one of the Congolese languages (Swahili); however in Kinyarwanda inyanya means tomatoes. At the market, I couldn't see the small aubergines that I was looking for so I approached a lady selling tomatoes and in a very broken Kinyarwanda mixed with Swahili, I asked her if she could direct me where nyanya were sold. Because to her inyanya meant tomatoes which were in front of us, she looked at me with complete shock and started shouting at me. I, on the other hand felt very stupid and ended up going home empty handed and upset.

Despite the difficulties, we settled quite well and started the new year of 1995 hoping that mama and the children were going to join us soon. The education system wasn't ready so we stayed at home doing housework and handcrafts.

MAMA'S MIRACULOUS JOURNEY

In mid January of 1995, we received a letter from a distant aunt who was still in Kisangani. In her letter, she explained how mama had become very ill and was in hospital. The situation was very serious because it was to do with her stomach and appendicitis. There was no money to afford the much needed surgery and her life was in danger. In her letter, aunty Bertha begged us to find ways of bringing mama to Rwanda for treatment and to be near us. Meantime she had contacted a few airlines to see if they could bring mama free of charge but none of them had replied to her letters. The following days saw papa trying his best to get money for mama's ticket but his efforts produced nothing. The bank declined his credit application and most of our new found extended family were too poor to help. We were left with no other option but prayer for another miracle. Papa had started saving but it would take him at least a couple of years before getting enough money for the flight tickets. I despaired because this time I could see no way out. I cried every night because I was scared very much to lose mama in what seemed to be a very far away land. I couldn't imagine life without her. I wondered what would happen to my poor little brothers and sister Charlotte who were now living with Aunty Bertha.

Three weeks after receiving Aunty Bertha's letter, it was around five thirty in the afternoon and the sun was getting ready to set. I was cooking dinner with my sisters helping when we heard some noises; papa and one of my aunties came escorting a woman with two children. She looked thin, darker and had short hair. For a moment I thought it was just another friend or family member until I realised it was mama and my younger sister and brother. We all ran towards them. We hugged and kissed her, crying like children. How on earth could I have believed that mama and two siblings were with us? She looked weak, tired and traumatised. In Congo, things had gotten worse since we left. Her illness made things even more difficult. Luckily one of the companies that Aunty Bertha contacted offered to bring mama and two children. My brother Emmanuel however was left to live with Aunty Bertha. It was the hardest decision mama had to make, to leave her son behind. I had never been so happy in my life. To see almost the whole family together in Rwanda was just a miracle. I do believe in miracles because they happened to us. There were now three members of our family left in Kisangani; my brother, my paternal grand-mama and uncle Celestin. Grand-mama and uncle were even poorer than us so they too counted on papa for help. We didn't know when we could afford to bring them.

The following day, we took mama to the local hospital where she was given treatment. Within a few weeks, she felt and looked better. She was so pleased to see some of her family, in particular her cousin who had taken her to Kisangani. It was almost eighteen years since she had last seen her and her family because they had moved to Burundi. My maternal grandparents and families whom we had never met before were still in Masisi, Congo. Tensions and conflict between Hutu militias, local rebels and Tutsi refugees in Masisi were very high. Dozens of people were killed each month. They included one of my uncles. Uncle Innocent was a businessman who travelled to neighbouring towns to buy merchandise in bulk. That day he and his friends had gone to buy palm oil. On their way back they met with a group of Hutu militia who ruthlessly attacked them. He and some of his friends were killed instantly. A few of his friends who had managed to escape the barbaric attack brought the tragic news home to his wife and seven children. Auntie Elizabeth was devastated. Her husband was the main bread winner. With seven young children it was going to be very hard for her to cope. Twelve years on, the family is still finding it hard to cope without him.

However, negotiations between Rwanda, Congo and the UNHCR about the refugees of Masisi began so there was some hope that they would come to Rwanda one day.

NO SCHOOL

I had just completed the first term of the sixth year of secondary school when we moved to Rwanda. Attending school was at the heart of my life because I knew that without education, I was not going to achieve much. My plan was to become a doctor or a pharmacist. I had chosen maths, chemistry, biology and chemistry for the equivalent of my A-level. When we arrived in Rwanda the education system was still disordered and soon after that, the government introduced an allocation system for secondary school students. Students had to apply at the ministry of education. Once the ministry allocated you a school, you had no choice but to accept the offer unless you had financial means to pay for a private school. Fees for public schools were far less compared to private ones. With five children at home, it was going to be a struggle for papa to afford the school fees. But he was very determined to put us through school. Every day I had to go to the ministry of education to find out which school I would attend. After weeks of waiting, I learned that I was going to be sent to a school in Nyamasheke, Cyangugu. At the time of my admission, the area was famous for militia attacks particularly in boarding schools like the one I was going to attend. There had already been many attacks and killings in boarding schools. Even though I had heard how notorious the place was, I still felt that I had to go because I couldn't contemplate life without studying. But the risks were too great. At home mama and papa made it clear that I couldn't attend school in such a dangerous area. However papa felt great responsibility for educating me because I was reaching the end of my secondary education and was doing really well.

"Maybe we should keep your brothers and sisters at home for just a year so that we can afford paying for a private school for you" the family suggested as we sat together trying to come up with alternatives.

"How could I possibly study with the knowledge that my brothers and sisters can't go to school because of me" I replied. "I am older than them and at least I am semi literate with the level of education that I have so please let us give them a chance. Mama! Papa! at nineteen I'm old enough to look for a job and support papa as he tries to meet our needs. Plus my brother is still in Kisangani. This could be our chance to get enough money to buy him a ticket so that he too can join us. Also if I get a good job, perhaps I could save some money and go to a private school afterwards".

Although the rest of the family thought it was a good idea, papa was very reluctant to allow me to work because, rightly enough, he felt that my dream of becoming a doctor would be shattered. He also felt that I was too young to take responsibility for his family.

"Well, I don't see any other way so I would rather work than stay at home" I said, as I tried my best to persuade papa that working was beneficial for all of us.

After hours of discussion, he finally agreed to let me look for a job. The conditions were that I worked locally, living at home and staying away from the youth madness which could easily steal my dream of further education.

"Yes papa, I will be the best young person you've ever seen" I said excitedly as I jumped on to him to give him a great big hug.

I knew that the best thing besides studying was to get a job in order to help mama and papa financially. I suddenly felt grown up and mature because finally my parents had trusted me enough to allow me to work, which was contrary to their usual overprotective behaviour. That night I couldn't sleep thinking how I had been given the chance of a lifetime to try and make my family better. Even though I didn't have a clue where the job was going to come from, I couldn't help but imagine what I would do with the money that I was going to earn. My priority was to help my brother join us. After the miraculous travel for most of us, my brother was left in Kisangani because we couldn't afford to bring him. It was the toughest decision that mama had to make; to leave him behind but she had no choice at the time as she was too ill not to accept the free flight offer for her and the two younger children to join us in Rwanda. So my brother was left to stay with Aunty Bertha. Our priority was to bring him but with my father's meagre salary, it was impossible.

I also imagined a shopping list. Items to shop for included a double bed for my parents because it bothered me very much to see them sleep in a single bed. I hated it. We kids needed a proper bed too. We slept on grass mattresses which were very uncomfortable but better than sleeping on the floor or on a mat. Because of the lack of proper bed sheets, the dry grasses use to pierce through and scratch our skin as we slept. On top of that mosquitoes were always there to make sure that we did not get the best of our sleep. It was awful but to us it was normal. So another item on my imaginary shopping list was a mosquito net for all of us. We needed a sofa too. Oh! and lots of clothes and hygienic stuff which we hadn't been able to afford. The list went on and on until I finally fell asleep.

The next morning I was away hunting for a job. I went from office to shops looking for any kind of job. I was very naïve. I thought that I could just go, ask and get a job. I soon discovered that it wasn't like that at all. My weeks of extensive search ended in vain. I felt frustrated, angry and very disappointed. The excitement and hope that I had when I was allowed to work turned into discouragement and hopelessness.

"My child, don't give up! Something will turn up one day," mama would often say, to see if she could lift me out of my misery.

After a few months I gave up the search for a job and stayed at home helping mama with the housework and spending free time visiting the many members of my extended family whom I did not know until we came to Rwanda. They were scattered all over Rwanda. After cleaning people's houses, they would pay me a small amount which paid for my transport.

In February 1995 I went to visit one of my maternal uncles in Gisenyi, a three hour trip from Kigali. I was very excited because it was where we had first landed when we came to Rwanda. It also meant that I was going to be near my darling country of birth which I was missing a great deal. Uncle Ubald worked in the local government. His job involved him with many non-governmental organisations such as the United Nations agencies and other charitable agencies. He was very pleased to see me. We spent the first few days visiting other family members who lived in rural areas. We had to climb mountains to reach some of them. I enjoyed meeting all these members of our extended family for the first time. I also loved going to the beach at Lake Kivu. The beach was beautiful. Across the road from the beach were the beautiful villas built by the lake. The breeze made the many palm trees' leaves wave gently. Local children loved escaping from the midday heat by diving and swimming into the lake. My enjoyment of the lake was limited to only watching them because I couldn't swim so couldn't join them.

A few days before my visit came to its end, I started an interesting conversation with my uncle. It was about my job search.

"I'm desperate to get a job uncle. I will do anything from cleaning to receptionist," I said.

"Right, I will see what I can do," he said.

Deep down in my heart, I knew that papa would not agree to let me work away from home but there was no way I was going to decline my uncle's offer for help. My holiday ended without getting the job I had hoped for; however there were one or two promises.

"You go back home and as soon as I hear from prospective employers, I will call your papa to let you know," he said.

"Thanks uncle," I said gratefully, showing that I was counting on him.

At home, I shared the news with the family. Just as I'd envisaged, papa wasn't very keen to let me work away. Mama and I had a hard time trying to persuade him that it was okay for me to work away. Papa was very protective. He always wanted the best for me and he found it very hard to trust teenagers perhaps because we lived in an environment where the rate of teenage pregnancies was quite high. Often young mothers found themselves stuck with no hope for further education because they became mothers at a young age.

FIRST JOB WITH INTERNATIONAL ORGANISATION FOR MIGRATION (IOM)

After a couple of weeks, my breakthrough happened; papa gave me the good news that my uncle had found me a job with the International Organisation for Migration (IOM). The organisation was responsible for the migration of hundreds of thousands of refugees returning to Rwanda from neighbouring Congo. Refugees returning to Rwanda travelled in big trucks. A truck usually carried up to 60 refugees at a time. My job was to clean these trucks. There were a couple of dozen of the trucks. I was to join a team of three people. They wanted me to start as soon as possible.

After a few days preparing myself for my new life, I packed and left for Gisenyi in March 1995. My uncle had a big house and a room for me - one of the reasons why my parents allowed me to work there. They knew that I would have adult supervision. They wrote me a book of instructions and of the dos and don'ts. We agreed that I would visit every last weekend of the month. On the way, I was very excited and nervous too. It was the first time I was going to stay away from home. The feeling and sense of freedom was fabulous. It was my chance to explore life without the strict eyes of my parents watching over me.

"Whatever I do, I must stick to papa and mama's advice" I kept reminding myself.

The strictest advice/instruction I received from them was to avoid boys and their romantic approaches. Unlike many young people in Africa, I was very lucky to have parents who were very open with us. They openly spoke to us about sex and its consequences. At that time, I used to feel rather embarrassed by the whole talk but I now appreciate very much their openness on this topic because I strongly believe that it averted major disasters from happening such as early pregnancy and the infection of Sexually Transmitted Diseases such as HIV Aids.

Security in Gisenyi and Ruhengeri was the country's biggest problem. Gisenyi shared the border with Congo from where militia and Hutu rebels used to attack Rwanda. Mines were planted and attacks on civilians often took place at night or early in the mornings.

On one of the many tragic incidents, I lost a close uncle when the bus he was on was attacked and burnt by militia. I loved Uncle Ruberwa very much. He wasn't much older than me so we used to joke a lot. I would often annoy him by asking when he was getting married to the girl next door. He was really the best uncle. When he'd arrived from Congo, he came to live with us in Gisenyi. Uncle Ruberwa then got a job with the beer factory located on the outskirts of the city. Each morning he would get on the workers' bus to go to work. Then one morning I heard on the radio that the workers' bus which was on its way to the factory had been attacked and most passengers were killed. The time and description of the bus sounded like the one uncle usually got on. I panicked and was shaken when I heard the news. Before phoning auntie Bernadette whom I knew would have the news by now, I prayed that uncle would have missed the bus or been absent from work that day. If not, my other prayer was that he would be amongst a couple of people who had managed to escape from the horrendous attack. However my worst nightmare came true when auntie Bernadette confirmed that uncle Ruberwa was amongst the dead. I sobbed on the phone like a child. I could feel the pain cutting through my heart like a sharp knife. The entire family and in particular his mama who dearly loved him was shocked and shaken by the tragic news. We missed him terribly. He was one of the hundreds of people to have lost their lives through these cold-blooded militia attacks.

As a result of these attacks, I wasn't allowed to be out after certain hours. Roads to Kigali were very dangerous too. Often cars and buses were stopped by militia who looked like the army. They would order everyone out and once they were out, they would then kill them. One unforgettable tragic incident was when I'd missed a bus and took the next one, only to discover that the bus I'd missed was attacked and most passengers were killed. These attacks used to petrify me but when you've no choice then life has to go on.

I arrived in Gisenyi on 10th March 1995 and started my job on the following day. On the first day, I met with Jean Louis, a French national who was the operations manager. After a small and quite an informal interview, he said to me "you've got the job". My heart beat rates must have gone through the roof. I could not believe my luck. He paused to look at my ecstatic face before continuing.

"You will start this evening. There are two shifts and we would like you to work on both of them. The morning one starts at five and ends at eight in the morning; the evening shift starts at six till nine in the evening. Tomorrow, Mr Pius the manager will discuss the terms and conditions with you. Do you have any questions?"

"No sir. Thank you very much sir. I am really grateful for you to have given me this job" I said almost shaking with disbelief.

"Now, let me show you where the trucks park and where you will be cleaning them."

That evening I returned to start my job. I met my three colleagues who were very good. I looked forward to doing the job and felt very blessed to have one. But the first few hours in my job proved harder than what I had thought. Climbing the trucks was not easy and the smell, filth and dirt inside them made the job even harder. Refugees left all sorts of dirt and mess in the trucks. But it was a job that many wished they had so I had to get on with it. I cleaned about six trucks on my first night.

"Not bad for a newcomer" cheered my colleagues.

Joking and laughing was their way of coping with their not so pleasant job. It wasn't long before I too joined them in jokes.

The following morning, I was asked to stay back so that I could speak to the organisation's manager. When I went to his office, he wasn't like the person I had imagined him to be. I had heard about him before; about his shouting when things went wrong. A very task orientated manager with perfect time management. After hearing the stories, I imagined he was a huge man with a big voice. Instead I saw a little man with a soft voice.

Speaking French with a very strong Italian accent he said

"Welcome to our organisation. I understand you started yesterday and I hope you're enjoying working with us."

"Yes sir" I fearfully replied.

He then presented me with the written terms and conditions which didn't mean much to me because I had the job and that was what mattered. I was curious to know my salary. I expected around US$30 to US$40 per month. You can imagine my joy when I found out that I was going to earn US$60 per month. It was beyond my imagination. I was so grateful to GOD for another miracle, grateful to the organisation which had given me the job, grateful to my uncle who persuaded them to employ me and very grateful to my parents who had allowed me to work away. I was just so, so happy. I left Mr Pius's office jumping and leaping with joy.

Business people were always going to Kigali so it made it easier to communicate with my family. We kept in-touch through writing and telephone because papa had a phone at work. They were very pleased to hear about my job and pay. The money was going to help us very much. But first, we had to get my brother out of Congo before it was too late. I decided to save at least $40 for five months so that I could get him a ticket. Even though it wasn't easy to save with so many other expenses at home, I felt I had no choice but to do so. At the end of the first month, I went home with my first salary. Papa and mama were very proud when I showed them the money. However there was very much poverty around so I failed to save for my brother's ticket as I had hoped but promised myself to stick to the plan the next time.

The second month into my job, I met a handsome young man who asked me for a date. With my parents' advice at the back of my mind, I accepted and agreed to meet him at the Palm Beach restaurant; a beautiful restaurant located near the beautiful Lake of Kivu. After the meal, we went for a walk along the lake. Somehow we ended up at the borders between Rwanda and Congo. It wasn't very busy so we decided to chat to the soldiers guarding the borders. Just as we were chatting, we saw a young man coming out of the immigration office. I nearly collapsed when I realised it was my brother. You would think by now I was used to miracles but each one bore a special surprise. I had just mentioned about my brother to my friend so he couldn't believe it either. We hugged and thanked God for the coincidence because he didn't know what he was going to do for overnight accommodation.

"How did you get here? I asked.

"I got a lift on the cargo."

Unbelievable! The whole family came through lifts on the cargo.

"Where were you going to stay tonight?" I asked

"I was planning to sleep rough tonight and get on the bus to Kigali tomorrow. Once in Kigali, I was planning to go to Mr Munka's shop at the bus station to locate you. How is everyone?"

Before I could reply, he jumped in with another question, "by the way what are you doing here? I thought the whole family was in Kigali."

"Yes, we were all in Kigali until I got a job here."

And then I remembered to introduce my friend Albert. As they chatted, I went and got a taxi and we went to my uncle. At home, he was very surprised to see Emmanuel. The next day, I put him on the bus to Kigali. I phoned papa from work to say that Emmanuel was on his way. Papa was understandably ecstatic over the phone. So that was how my whole family moved to Rwanda. Amazing!!!!!!!!!!!!

PROMOTION

At work, Mr Pius the manager would, now and again, pop in to see how we were doing. I was lucky to be fluent in French which made communication easy for me, unlike my colleagues who struggled to understand him. I often stepped in to interpret if there was something important to announce. My colleagues feared Mr Pius very much. As soon as he appeared, staff would almost freeze as if they had just seen a god. Even though I feared him to some extent, it never stopped me from chatting to him freely. It was during these conversations that he learned about my background and school level.

Almost four months into my job, he asked me to see him in his office after my morning shift. I couldn't understand why he wanted to see me in his office and started thinking the worst. "Is it bad news or good news?" I kept asking myself. Soon after the end of my shift, I went to his office. His pleasant mood reassured me.

"There is a vacancy for a field worker in the organisation and we think you are suitable for it" he said.

My thoughts were; *"Oh my God! This can only be another dream and this time the dream has gone too far."*

Field workers worked directly with refugees returning from Congo. Field workers assisted them from their arrival at the Rwandan border to their settlement into communities. There were transit camps in rural areas where they were transported to before settling them into society according to their place of origin. I knew I would love the job because it meant travelling a lot in those posh 4X4 UNHCR jeeps in order to go to different camps and settlement villages. Field workers also liaised with the government authorities and many other different organisations such as UNDP, UNICEF, World Food Organisation, World Vision, Save the Children, Red Cross, Care etc which was great. Plus it meant my salary would jump from US$60 to US$110 per month. I accepted the job offer expressing my true and genuine gratitude to Mr Pius. I was to start the following week. My colleagues were happy for me even though I felt awful for having to leave them for a promotion when they had been there much longer than me. I presumed my fluency in French had made me more suitable for the job because communication with the many foreign workers was vital. I was now going to work from eight o' clock in the morning to six o' clock in the evening. I phoned papa for the good news and on hearing about my promotion, he was very pleased but joked saying that I would now be earning a lot more than him and that I would now become the big boss at home.

"But, I shall keep my paternal authority and power" he jokingly said.

The week of my start couldn't come quickly enough and before I knew it, it was time to join my new team of field workers. It was a big department with one local staff as deputy manager and a French expatriate as operations manager. The induction week was great because I was introduced not only to my colleagues but to some foreign and government staff as well. After the induction week, I started my new job going to the border to register returnees and escorting them to the transit refugee camps where they had to be assessed. The increase in salary meant that I was now able to realise most of my short term dreams. So, month after month, I accumulated furniture that was badly needed at home, including a double bed for my parents and other things. It also meant that the financial burden at home was much reduced. The family was in the position to pay for school fees not only for the five children but for other children orphaned by the war. It was such a pride and joy to take my salary home each month. We even managed to buy two flight tickets for grand-mama and uncle Celestin who were still in Kisangani. However the lady who took them from Rwanda was caught in the intense civil war at the Bangoka airport in Kisangani. The tickets were confiscated and either sold or destroyed. She was arrested and beaten but somehow managed to escape from the torture. The fate of grand-mama and uncle was now in God's hands and thank God that a few months later they managed to come to Rwanda through a UNHCR repatriation programme. Grand-mama's legs were paralysed because she had to sit in the same position for six months in the tiny hideout where they were hidden in order to escape from the killing of Rwandans which had intensified in Congo.

HELLO GRANDPAPA!

"Mr Pius my grandparents, aunties, uncles and cousins, whom I've never met, will be amongst the refugees arriving from Masisi today. It will be hard for me to work because I want to meet and get to know them."

"Of course you can't work today so take the day off" he kindly said.

It had been months since the government of Rwanda had started to negotiate with the UNHCR about returning the refugees of 1961 who lived in Masisi, a town near the city of Goma in eastern Congo. The vast majority of the much grown Rwandan community there couldn't afford the costs of coming to Rwanda after more than thirty years in exile. The minority of people who could afford to pay for the transport had constant fear for their lives because there were known to be rebels in the vast forest on the way to Rwanda who had killed many people on previous occasions. Most of these veteran refugees were stuck in this unsecured zone until UNHCR agreed to bring them under a military convoy. The operation took weeks because refugees returning to Rwanda were in their thousands. A convoy could take up to a week before reaching Rwanda. We were always told in advance which town or village was next for arrival so I knew exactly when mama's family would be coming. But when they arrived, there were about three to four thousands of them.

After hours of trying to locate them amongst the returnees, I finally came across them for the first time - no one can describe the feeling that went through me when I first set my eyes on my grandpa. Even though we hadn't met before, we used to regularly write to each other and the letter between grandpa and I always began with the line "to my fiancé grandpa" or "to my fiancée Chantal". This is because in some part of Africa, a granddaughter pretends to be her grandfather's bride and a grandson pretends to be his grandmother's groom. It is a joke aimed at having fun between grandparents and their grandchildren. I always felt very close to him even though I had never met him before - it was a dream come true to finally meet him. As I lifted my eyes to where they pointed me of their location, I saw a man looking frail sitting on a dirty bag, leaning on his stick.

"Hello grandpapa!" I said.

"Who are you?" he quietly replied as the long and difficult journey had made him very tired and frail.

"I am Chantal Batamuriza, the daughter of Collette your daughter" I said with tears flowing down my cheeks. Grandpa didn't look like what I had imagined. I'd never seen his photo before so I had only an imagined what he looked like. He was tall and dark. Even at that age, he gave me the impression that he was a very handsome man.

Just when he was about to hug me, I was pulled by the elderly lady sitting beside him, speechless for a few moments, they both hugged me for quite a long time thinking that they were dreaming.

All they could say was, "Collette was your age when she left, and it's a miracle to see her child for the first time, at the same age that she left us. Where is she?" they both asked, but, before I could give them the answer, I was pulled here and there by different aunts, uncles and cousins, whom I had never met before. It was very emotional. In a moment, I'd gained a big family that I had never met before.

"Are we going with you?" they asked eagerly.

"Not now," I said. "You have to go through the procedure of registration so that you will be given land by the government" I explained.

"So where are we going to stay? When are we going to see your mother and the rest of your family?"

"Soon" I said as I led them to the registration desk.

Moments later they were transported to the transition camp. Because I often worked there, I saw them every day. After a week, they were allowed to go to Kigali to meet my family. I travelled with them to Kigali and as we arrived home, celebrations began. Tears of joy and hours of getting to know each other followed. We had about thirty people in our two bed-roomed house. It was very crowded but great. After a week, they went to stay in the countryside where a plot with a hut in it had been given to them by the government. Grandpapa died in 1996 and grandmama died a year later. It was a very happy ending for them to have seen us and to have been buried in their homeland.

NO MORE JOB

I was enjoying every second of my job. I met many people and made many new friends. I felt proud to be helping my people resettle after such a long time in exile. I met with all sots of people from immigration officials to NGOs staff.

My joy of working however was cut short when after turning down a date with my line manager, it resulted in him making my work hell. My boss had asked me out and I declined as I could not imagine me dating him. He was married with children almost my age. He started to make up rules so that I would be affected and started to harass me. I mentioned the situation to a couple of colleagues who advised me to just get on with it because the management would have probably done nothing much about it. My colleagues had previously been harassed by him and just ignored him. But weeks later I could hardly take it any more so I resigned. My liaison with many organisations meant that I had a chance to apply to them. I applied for jobs with many organisations but with no success.

Disappointed and feeling crushed, I headed back to Kigali. Before leaving, I collected as many Head Office addresses as possible because most of them were located in Kigali. My friend John of British Direct Aid gave me their Head Office address in Kigali so that I could try my luck there but he warned me that I must first learn English before attempting to apply with the organisation. Many of the organisation's expatriate staff were British who hardly spoke any language other than English. The fear of telling the truth to my uncle and family about not having a job made me tell them that I had a job offer in Kigali and that I was moving there to be close to my family. At home, they were thrilled at my imaginary news. My father in particular was very relieved to have me back by his side. I told my family that I was on a two week holiday before starting my new job. They trusted me enough not to ask too many questions. Two weeks meant I had enough time to intensely hunt for a job. I applied to many organisations without any success.

SECOND JOB WITH BRITISH DIRECT AID (BDA)

After failing to secure a job with other NGOs, I went to the British Direct Aid offices to try my luck. British Direct Aid was an organisation that supported the UNHCR in its massive repatriation and resettlement operations. The organisation was in charge of the biggest garage in Kigali which oversaw the repair of all UNHCR vehicles. Its operations also included the complex distribution of fuel to United Nations cars and the distribution of drinking water to United Nations and Government organisations. It employed up to twelve British expatriates and over fifty local staff, mainly mechanics. As I left home that morning, I was very determined not to go home without a job, because my two weeks leave was soon going to end so I had no choice but find a job. Even though my English was very broken I knew that they would understand me. If not then I hoped there would be a French speaking person. The garage was huge and had plenty of space around it. Some of the United Nations' cars were parked outside. At the gates, the security person checked my United Nations Identification card which I had kept with me for allowing me easy access into NGOs buildings.

"Who do you want to speak to?" he asked after checking my card.

"I would like to speak to the general manager please" I said.

"He is under that pick up" he said as he pointed to where the vehicle was.

I approached the vehicle and saw someone under it. I could not believe my eyes when I leaned down and saw a white man under the car, meaning that actually the big boss was under it. *"I expected a local staff member under this car not a British manager!"* I thought to myself.

"Hello" I said.

At this, he came out in his overall darkened by perhaps the oil and grease of the car that he was fixing.

"Hello, can I help you" he said.

By this time I was digging in my memory for the school English that I had learned in order to make myself understood.

"Me name Chantal" I said. It took me several seconds to put the next phrase together.

"Me work IOM Gisenyi. John BDA Gisenyi friend" I continued after much effort trying to explain that I knew John of BDA Gisenyi.

He patiently waited, I suppose wanting to know where this conversation was leading to. "Gisenyi work finish, me no job. Family big problem. No job, no money, no food, big problem. Me job here, boss please job here now"

After I finished speaking he tried his best to confirm that he had no job for me.

"Boss me clean here"

"Please boss, me no job, me no go home."

He soon found out that he wasn't going to get rid of me easily so he resumed his work. However I sat there all the time following him wherever he went. He was so gentle and so patient that he never shouted nor showed his frustration towards me. The day passed and I went home. I could not sleep. "Where was the job going to come from?" I asked myself. The next day, I was first at the BDA garage. This time, I could not pass the gates so I sat at the gates all day.

After a few days of waiting at the gates, the manager called me. He took me to the fuel distribution point where a tall dark man was working. The gentleman spoke English and so interpreted for me.

"Tell her that I got a job for her" he said.

I could understand the word job so I hoped it was good news. When the man interpreted what he had just said, my heart melted with joy. I was going to assist Peter with distributing fuel to UN vehicles. I was grateful to the manager and expressed my thanks. I have since learned that he is an Earl and a Peer in the House of Lords. My heartfelt thanks to him for having given me the job that changed my life.

I started immediately. My job was to pump fuel into the vehicles and record the information on a fuel supply sheet. At the end of the day, I would pass on all the forms to Peter who would in turn report to the Operations Manager who was British. My first work related English lesson began on that day because the form that had to be completed was in English. My colleague Peter was very helpful. After a few days I was told that my salary would be US$30 per week. I was overjoyed because I was worried about earning less than my previous salary which would have meant explaining myself to my family.

During my brief visits to the office, I came closer to computers and my curiosity of how they functioned increased. One day when I went to the office, the manager was not at his desk. As I sat there waiting for him, I was fascinated by the screensaver that was on. I watched the three D objects going round and coming forward. I loved it. I wanted to see what would happen if I touched the keyboard so I did - suddenly the computer's screen changed and I panicked because I thought that I'd broken something. When the boss came, I was quick to apologise and said to him "I think I broke your machine. I touched a button here and it changed, I'm really sorry if I have broken it".

I was surprised by his smiley face because I expected him to be mad at me.

He knew that my English was not good so in broken French he gently explained to me how the computer worked. The look on my face must have amused him. It was fascinating to see the spreadsheet and how fuel reports were recorded into Microsoft Access. I could not believe it when I saw the computer adding up everything so accurately. I was very interested in learning how the computer worked that my boss agreed to spend a few minutes with me every day to learn how to record my fuel reports on the computer and I loved doing it. The office administration team only had one local staff (Martin) who spoke very good English. The rest of the team were white British. Martin's job varied from arranging for expatriates' visas and work permits to interpreting for other staff who didn't speak English. The rest of the local staff worked as mechanics, cleaners or fuel attendants. I envied Martin's position because he got to mix with white people. He was like the link officer between the British expatriates and local staff. He was also like the external relations manager. He had a walkie talkie and a chauffeur driven company car. He was also in charge of ensuring that our salaries were paid on time. Most of us didn't have bank accounts so we were paid in cash at the personnel office. At the end of the month,

Martin used to withdraw a large sum of money from the bank and bring it to the office for our wages. He withdrew more than US$20,000 each month.

I didn't like Martin from the day I met him. He was a small man who came across as an angel but I could tell his manners hid another side of him. He was calm but arrogant. He thought that because he was in charge, we had to do everything he said even when it didn't make sense. Like my previous boss, he too had asked me to go out with him and I declined, so from that day our working relationship became horrible. I never felt comfortable around him because he never gave up about me going out with him. It almost became like sexual harassment but this time I could not risk resigning so I just had to put up with him. This horrible working relationship went on for months and made my work feel like hell. Luckily he worked in the office and I worked outside in the fuel place, so the only time he saw me was when I went to the office to hand in fuel reports or when he came to give us instructions.

ANOTHER PROMOTION!

It was the end of the month and we were expecting to be paid our salary. That afternoon we were all called for a special meeting with the management. It wasn't good news - Martin had disappeared with our money. It was a lot of money, probably between US$20,000 and US$25,000. No one knew where he was. The police were called and investigations immediately started. The disappearance of Martin and the money meant late payment for us and a big loss for the organisation. He was never caught. Everyone was shocked because he seemed trustworthy.

A few weeks after the disappearance of Martin, I was called into the office by our new manager. The manager who had given me the job had left so Christopher from England became our new manager. He was slim, tall and very white and I liked his accent. He spoke slowly and clearly. I'd learned a few new words which helped me understand some of his English. He spoke a bit of French so our conversation was always mixed between English and French. On my way to his office, I couldn't think of the reason he had called me. In his office I nervously sat at the chair where he'd shown me to sit.

"Following Martin's disappearance there is now a vacancy in the office" Mr Barley said. We think you are suitable for the job and we would like to offer you the post".

Making sure that I understood every word, he took his time to speak slowly and clearly. Where I didn't quite understand him, he would try in French. After explaining the role and job involved, I couldn't believe my luck. This could only be described as another miracle because the job was posh; I expected people with perfect English and a degree in Administration to have this job. "How on earth could they trust a young girl with broken English to do this job?" I wondered. The post's salary was about $190 per month. It was hard to believe that I was now going to be earning a lot more than a head of a department in the government ministry. I accepted the job offer with pleasure but deep down my heart I knew it was a great challenge because my English was incomplete. Luckily I worked with locals more than I did with my British colleagues. I only spoke to my British managers during reporting time. My new line manager was Diane. I didn't know Diane well because I hadn't worked directly with her in the past. However, I knew that she seemed nice and full of life. Whenever she brought her 4X4 land rover for fuel, she nicely spoke to all of us. She easily connected with local staff and I later found out why - she was born and partly brought up in Africa so she had a special bond with Africans. As the general manager introduced me to Diane as her new office clerk; I felt that we would get on well. She welcomed me with open arms and became not only my line manager but my mentor and best friend.

MEETING MY STEP BROTHER FOR THE FIRST TIME

"You won't believe what happened today" papa said as he walked towards the sitting room looking quite drunk not only by the alcohol that he'd been consuming but by the news he was about to tell us. Papa loved going to the local pub in the evenings. He'd met different people but this time he'd met a special person.

"What? Mama curiously asked as we all gathered to hear this big news.

"Today I met Samson who was my best friend in the fifties and he knows where my son is"

"Wow, that's amazing" mama said

We were all amazed at the news that finally we were in the position to trace my step brother whom we had never met before. I'm glad papa mentioned about the potential existence of his child t to us otherwise we would've been deeply shocked by the news.

Our step brother Christopher, had been born and raised in Uganda where his mother had settled since she left Rwanda. Christopher was living with his partner and had a daughter. I was suddenly an auntie and our family gained another member in minutes. Papa didn't want to shock his son by visiting him so he wrote instead. Unable to say much in the letter, he kept it brief and promised to meet him as soon as he replied to his letter. As we waited for Christopher's reply, I became nervous at the same time. For days, thoughts raced through my mind:

What does it feel to meet your step brother for the first time?
What does he look like? Does he look like papa?

What if he doesn't like us?
What if he doesn't speak our language?
What will be his reaction and ours when we meet him?
What if he blames papa for what happened?

Within weeks most of my questions were answered when instead of writing a letter my step brother came to meet us. I'd just arrived from work and was having a cold drink when I heard some noises outside. When I went outside to investigate I saw papa with his photocopy. My step brother looked like he was papa's twin with only the age difference being obvious. I have never seen anyone in my family resemble papa like my brother Chris. As soon as I came out, papa cheerfully presented me to my brother, who like me was understandably over the moon to meet us. His reaction and eagerness to know us made it easier for us to get on very well with him. The whole family was in tears of joy. He spent a few days with us telling us his side of the story and listening to ours. In a moment my family became a family of seven instead of six. We were proud of him to have achieved so much without his papa's presence. From that day we visited each other as often as possible. His cute little girl was equally pleased to have so many aunties and uncles. He married his partner and the whole family travelled to Uganda for the wedding and he was very proud to have us by his side at his wedding. We met his mother; a wonderful woman who loved God and people very much. She jokingly said to mama that she had stolen her would be husband.

Sadly in November 2004 and almost a year after his mother's death, we lost our step brother Christopher to a motorbike accident. It has been very hard without him and we miss him terribly. He was the best brother and will always be in our thoughts. I'm thankful that I got to meet and know him even though it was for a short period. He has left us two beautiful children, Brenda and Allan, and a wonderful sister in law, Jane.

FIRST TRIP TO SCOTLAND

"What's your biggest dream?" Diane asked as we sat at the Greek restaurant for my twenty first birthday. I'd never been to such a beautiful restaurant before. Like I said above, Diane was my manager but quickly became my best friend. My efforts to improve my broken English fascinated her. She often laughed loud before correcting me. She was one of the muzungus (whites) that I was never embarrassed to talk to in my broken English. I dearly loved her. We often went for a tea break in posh hotels and restaurants. She made me feel special. Both her and her husband had worked for British Direct Aid since 1994. The couple were from Scotland. I knew very little about Scotland but Diane taught me a lot about her country.

"I would love to gain a degree in office management" I replied.

"You see, it was my dream to become a doctor but at twenty one, I feel it is too late to achieve my dream. However I am enjoying office work very much and I feel geared towards learning more about office and management, but due to family commitments I'm unable to pursue my dream of further education just now."

Diane carefully listened to my story. She was very touched. Feeling emotional she held my hands, looked me in my eyes and said

"When I go back home to Scotland, I promise to help you achieve your goal of studying. I will sponsor you to come and study in my country."

I couldn't believe my ears, it was a miracle to hear Diane's promises. I knew that she meant every word she said because she's a lady of integrity and good character. I hugged her and said:

"When this happens - it will be a double dream come true because studying in Europe will be a bonus."

Having a white person to sponsor you come to Europe or North America is every young African's dream. So you can imagine my family's joy when I told my parents that Diane had promised to sponsor me. My family sometimes invited Diane and John for traditional Rwandan meals and they enjoyed it. Whenever Diane and John came home I had to interpret for my family in my broken English. We had wonderful times.

Like many other foreign workers, Diane and John's contracts were temporary. Their contracts ended in October 1996. We organised a farewell party for them and a few other British workers who were leaving at the same time. Deep down in my heart, I hoped to see the McGowans again one day, this time not in Africa but in Britain. What a dream!

At the airport, Diane hugged me and said,

"See you in Scotland".

"Yes! See you in Scotland" I confidently replied.

"Meantime we shall keep in-touch right?"

"Right" I replied.

As we waved goodbye, I felt empty because a great white boss and friend was leaving. No more rides in her white land rover with BDA logo; no more kilo bravo 7.6 as we knew her on her walkie talkie; no more going to posh restaurants etc. As much as it hurt seeing my friends leaving, it also brought hope for me to a much better future, because their departure meant sponsoring me to come to Europe.

At work, colleagues who knew about my close relationship with Diane could see that I was greatly missing her. They kept saying "well let hope that you will see her again soon because she is going to sponsor you to go to Scotland".

I knew that Diane would do it because as promised she kept in-touch with me, mainly by phone.

In January 1997, the management changed from British Direct Aid to a German organisation know as GTZ. Our senior managers were no longer British but Germans and Ethiopians. We missed the British managers because they were very gentle and patient. But we got on well with the new management too.

Eight months after Diane and her husband had left Rwanda and in June 1997, she told me that she was ready to invite me to Scotland.

"Are you serious?" I asked in disbelief.

"Of course I am serious" she replied.

After putting the phone down I was jumping up and down with excitement like a child. Within a few days she had faxed the invitation letter. Luckily I was already a passport holder so there was no delay in applying for the visa. However I found out that the British Consulate in Kigali did not cater for visa services so I had to travel to Uganda for the visa application which meant extra expense. I also needed to prove to the visa office that I'd a good amount of money in my bank account. Because I didn't have a lot of money, I got my friend to deposit some money into my bank account. With all documentation ready, I went to Kampala on an eight hours journey. I stayed with our friend's relative who told me to go to the visa office very early because otherwise there was no chance to make it to the first thirty. The visa office only took applications from the first thirty in the queue. The next day I was at the visa office by four thirty in the morning. It was still dark but there were only a dozen of us. By six o' clock, the queue had grown to almost a hundred. I don't know why people in the queue after thirty still waited because it was well known that the embassy only took the first thirty applications. The office gates opened at eight thirty and the security guard checked us before allowing us to go in. At the reception, we deposited our application forms and relevant documents. We were told to wait in the waiting area until our names were called. After forty minutes, I was called to pay the visa fees. I was told to wait for an interview with the immigration officer. Unofficial statistics show that more than half of the applicants are refused visas. I knew that I had a fifty-fifty chance of getting the visa. I waited for almost four hours before my name was called for an interview. The interview room looked like a bank cashier area with officers protected by the heavy glass that stood between the officer and the applicant. I suppose this was for safety reasons as some applicants could become violent and abusive when told their applications for a visa have been refused.

At the interview, I was very nervous not only because of the way the officer looked at me which intimidated me but also my English was not complete. *"How could she give me visa when I can't even express myself properly in her language?"* I wondered within myself. After the interview, she asked me to return at three o'clock in the afternoon. When I returned, my passport was ready for collection. I'd heard so many stories about people who'd been refused a visa so I wasn't sure what to expect. I was handed my passport as soon as I walked in at the reception. My hands were shaking when I opened it. I was so delighted to see that I was given a six month visitor's visa. *"Oh my God, my dream has practically come true."*

I went to the travel agent where I'd made a booking for my flight to London and paid for it. It was cheap for me to fly from Kampala to London. My flight was in a week's time so I returned home to Rwanda to prepare for my miraculous journey to Britain. People at home could not believe my luck. My work colleagues organised a party and it was great. Most people envied my position. They wished they had the visa and were flying to Britain. The atmosphere near my departure date was indescribable. It was such a privilege and great honour to be flying to Britain. Apart from my wedding day and the birth of my two sons, I cannot even think of any other day in my life I felt so excited and so over the moon. I had dreamed about Europe every day of my life so to be able to come was a lifetime opportunity.

On 19th of June 1997, papa and I left for Kampala so that he could see me off. I had over US$100 for spending money. We stayed in a hostel for a night because my flight was to leave from Entebbe on the following day. My flight to London was at three o clock in the afternoon via Nairobi. On the departure day, I put on my best outfit and we went to the airport. After quite an extensive check, I was given the boarding pass. After a big and emotional hug from papa, I entered the waiting room for passengers. Within an hour, we were asked to board the plane. Feeling a sense of pride, I walked towards the plane. People had spoken to me about how massive long haul planes are. I expected a huge plane but was surprised to see a small Boeing 707. However it was great to arrive inside a proper plane. It was very different from the cargo plane that I had boarded when going to Rwanda. This one felt more comfortable. It was also nice, clean and tidy. The Air hostesses were beautiful girls who spoke in posh English. I then sat in one of the chairs not knowing that I should have read my seat number. When the seat holder came, he appeared to be a little bit confused. After checking his seat number, one of the crew politely explained to me that I had occupied the wrong seat. I then apologised explaining that it was my first time on a proper flight. She then showed me where my seat was and kindly explained to me how it worked. I patiently waited for the plane to start moving and as soon as it did, it was as if my mind and body were moving too. All I could do was to imagine how exciting my trip was going to be. As the plane left the ground and flew higher up in the skies, I could see Lake Victoria far below us until it disappeared from my sight.

At Nairobi airport, I was told that my night flight to London was cancelled. There were about sixteen of us travelling to London. The flight company took us to a five star hotel in Nairobi. It was awesome! I had never been to a five star hotel before, never mind sleep in one. The room was massive and the self service dinner was presidential to me. Everything was like a dream, a sweet one. It was surreal.

The following morning, the waiting bus drove us to the airport. The immigration authorities questioned my visa but after providing them with genuine contact of my white sponsor, they allowed me to pass. As soon as I walked into the waiting room, I saw the massive plane through the glass windows. I'd never seen such a huge plane in my life. It was unreal.

"How could a huge plane like this fly?" I asked myself.

My thoughts must have come out loud because the person sitting next to me turned round and said

"Did you speak to me?"

"No" I quickly said. "I was just thinking about the huge plane outside."

He looked at me as if to say "yeah! Where are you from?"

After a few minutes, they called us through the loud speaker. It felt so good to be greeted and shown much respect at the plane's door. This time, I successfully located my seat in the massive plane and sat down. As I sat there waiting for the plane to take off, flashes of my past started to run through my mind like a video. *"Who, in their right mind would have thought that I, a girl from such extreme poverty, would be sitting in a long haul plane on my way to Britain? You had to be crazy or insane to think that I would be on my way to Europe one day."*

We left Nairobi at about eleven in the morning and arrived at Heathrow airport at around seven thirty in the evening. When the plane started to descend, I couldn't believe my eyes. The nearer to the ground we got, the clearer I could see all the buildings, the infrastructure, the airport etc and it all seemed like I had imagined. It was like watching a movie. The airport was vast. It was like a whole town/city in my country. Just when I was getting my hand luggage from the locker, I heard my name on the speakers.

"Would Miss Chantal Batamuriza please come forward to the front of the plane?" the announcement said.

At the front of the plane, I was met by one of the crew who then introduced me to a young lady. The lady worked for the immigration service; she had been asked by Diane to collect and help me with the checking procedure. She took me to the immigration desk and after all the formalities, I was allowed to go. Seeing so many white people was very strange and I felt like being inside a movie because that was where we got to see so many white people and tall buildings. After almost twenty minutes of wonders and disbelief, I finally remembered to phone my sponsor.

I needed help on how to work the public telephone. Luckily I am not the shy type; I believe in asking for help when you need it so I approached a gentleman who kindly showed me what to do. I soon found out that I needed some money to operate the public telephone. In Africa you pay the shop keeper before using the public phone; because these ones stood on their own, I had thought that it was free to use them. I went to exchange my dollars and received about £60. I then phoned Diane who was anxiously awaiting my arrival. After the initial excitement,

"Are you flying straight to Scotland?" she asked.

"No, I am catching a bus" I replied. I had planned to get a bus to Scotland and thought that it was not far from London.

When she heard about my plan, she became a bit nervous because she knew how confusing this could be to me, so she instructed me to go to the information desk in order to get more information. After locating the desk, I approached the lady and in broken English, I explained my situation. She then explained that there was no bus to Scotland that night.

"You should get a Bed & Breakfast to stay for the night and catch your bus tomorrow morning" she said. After finding out the meaning of Bed & Breakfast; I said,

"Where is a cheap Bed & Breakfast?"

"Kings cross" she said spontaneously.

"How do I go there?" I asked

"You need to take that lift" she replied pointing at it, "then go down to the ground floor and you will see the underground train which will take you to Kings cross ask anyone there and they will help you".

I did as she said and went on to the lift. Inside the lift, it took me a couple of minutes trying to work out how to get to the ground floor. Luckily someone else came in and rescued me by pressing the right button. On the ground floor, I saw something which to me looked like a waiting area. People were comfortably sitting and most of them were reading. The train looked too clean and modern to be a train; not that I had seen one. I went back upstairs and told the lady at the information desk that there was no train but people sitting in what seemed to me like a waiting area. She convinced me that was the right platform for trains so I went back downstairs again. The train had left. When I saw the rail tracks only then I believed that what I saw was actually a train. The next one arrived within minutes and I went in. It was my first time to see a train. It felt very different from the cars and planes that I had been on. It made a lot of noise and travelled faster than a car. By their looks, people seemed to be miles away from this world. It was as if everyone on the train had a lot on their mind. Others were reading. It was very different.

At Kings Cross, I asked for directions to the nearest Bed & Breakfast and someone kindly showed me. I paid £21 for the night and soon my money was fast reducing and I wondered if I would have enough for the bus ticket. The lady at the airport had given me a twenty four hour National Express coach helpline so I phoned. I soon discovered that I did not have enough money to pay for my ticket. I thought about asking the Bed & Breakfast to give me the money back but "where will I sleep?" I kept asking myself. I was scared and upset. I did not want to cause inconvenience to Diane by asking her to help. The trip which I was enjoying very much suddenly turned sour. After so much thinking, I decided to ring Diane and explain; after all she was the only person I knew. On the phone I nervously explained my situation to Diane. She was worried sick about the situation. She panicked a lot and took the B&B contact details and promised to call me as soon as she found a solution. After a couple of hours she phoned with good news.

"I have booked you on the British Midlands flight to Edinburgh" she said.

"Thank you very much Diane" I said relieved to hear the news.

"Your flight will leave tomorrow from Heathrow at eleven o' clock in the morning. You must be there by nine, right?"

"Yes madam" I gratefully said.

I could now sleep at peace. The following morning I went on the train to Heathrow. After checking in, I went to sit in the waiting area. However I sat in the wrong place. This waiting area was for British Airways. Because of the name British, I automatically thought that I was at the right place. As I sat there waiting for British airways passengers to be called for their flight to Edinburgh, I was surprised to see that by eleven o clock which was the flight time, they still did not call for British Airways passengers to board the plane. Even though passengers for my flight were called to board, I didn't pay any attention because to me it was British Airways. At eleven fifteen, I approached the receptionist who took a look at my ticket.

"My dear you are at the wrong place, wait here" she said as she called British Midlands office to tell them about me.

"We were just in the process of getting rid of her luggage before the plane took off. Ask her to run to the gate where the plane is".

The receptionist then said to me "come on, let's run before this plane leaves you behind."

We ran and ran. At the door the hostess said "Welcome Miss Batamuriza." It is as if she had memorised my name through the many announcements that were made in order to locate me, but somehow I heard none of them. It was quite embarrassing, because when I entered everyone in the plane looked at me as if to say *"because of you we are delayed."* On the other hand I felt quite important that a plane had waited over twenty minutes for me.

When we landed at Edinburgh airport, I expected to meet with my hosts inside the airport so you can imagine my surprise and joy when I came off the plane and saw Diane and her friend Rona on the tarmac holding a long, massive poster which read **"WELCOME TO SCOTLAND".** As I came down the plane, tears of joy were rolling down my cheeks. It was like a presidential reception. I dropped my hand luggage and ran to Diane, jumped on to her and gave her a great big hug which lasted many minutes. We were both in tears. She then introduced me to Rona. After checking my passport and visa, it was time to go home to Fife. I was very excited. The journey to Fife took longer than I had imagined. On the way, my eyes were wide open. The roads looked perfect and I was fascinated to see such a big, long bridge (Forth Road).

When we arrived, the houses looked normal, except the area, neighbourhood and gardens were much cleaner than what I was used to. Inside was a different story. The flat was immaculately decorated. Diane immediately gave me a tour of the house. My room had a double bed. It looked perfect. The bathroom was neat and tidy. I loved the sitting room too. In it, were a very comfy sofa, a big television with a video recorder and a huge Hi Fi - just what I'd been dreaming about in my life. The mother of all surprises lay in the kitchen. Seeing and learning about the washing machine was like seeing a magician. "How can a machine wash clothes?" I asked. I could not wait to see how it worked. And when it did, I sat besides it for the full wash, watching how it spun clothes to wash them. I was amazed to see that clothes were properly washed and almost dried.

After the tour, we sat for lunch and stories. Diane made some tuna, ham, cheese and tomatoes sandwiches. They tasted different because this was the first time I had eaten sandwiches. Back home, bread for those who can afford it is used for breakfast only so I was quite surprised to have bread at lunch time. It was lovely to meet Diane's children for the first time. Just as I had heard a lot about them, they too had heard a lot about me. At night time, I couldn't get used to my new bed because it was too comfortable. I couldn't sleep the first few nights. Thoughts of how great life seemed kept running through my mind. It took me a couple of days to actually realise that I was living the reality and not dreaming it. Diane and her husband had to go to work so I stayed home on my own. Unlike back home where I would have to wait until the next day to know what I would eat or in some cases whether I would eat at all, here the fridge was always full of food and drink. I ate and drank whenever I wanted to; I listened to music; I watched the television and loved the fact that there were so many channels that worked twenty four hours a day. I loved the hot full bath with bubbly crème. Water is very scarce at home so it was with great pleasure that I spent almost fifty to seventy minutes daily lying in the hot bath. Everyday I felt like a princess living in a palace. I wrote a nine page letter to my family describing my new found paradise.

Upon my arrival, I had asked Diane if there was a Christian church where I could go to worship. On Sunday, she took me to the local parish church. That day, the visiting minister was a gentleman who used to live in South Africa. He was very pleased to see me because it was extremely rare to come across Black Africans in this corner of Scotland. During the service, he called me to the front in order to greet me and let me introduce myself to the congregation. I gladly stood and went to the front. After introducing myself, I took the opportunity to demonstrate how we praise and worship at home. I sang, clapped my hands and danced at the same time. Suddenly the congregation joined me and started clapping theirs too. We all had fun. I was also pleased to hear the minister mention about the lively, full of fun ways that Africans do their praise and worship in his sermon. I noticed that it was different in the Church of Scotland.

At the end of the service, I was given some flowers. *"Wow! This is great! I'm really enjoying the attention that I am getting."* People at the church were very welcoming, friendly and really nice. I promised them to come back. However, one member didn't like the way I sang and danced in the church. He approached me and said:

"This is the house of God; you are not supposed to make a noise and dance like that; it isn't how we do it in our church."

"Well no wonder there aren't many young people in your church" I thought.

A week later, I returned to the church and attended its service every Sunday.

I also enjoyed the attention I got from many Fifers who had never seen a Black person before. They were fascinated by the colour of my skin and my afro hair. Children enjoyed touching my hair because it felt different. Some of them would rub my skin to see if the black colour would come off. It was such a different and strange experience!!

COLLEGE

A few weeks after my arrival, I was called for an interview at Glenrothes College following my application for High National Certificate in Administration and Information Management. Diane drove me to the place. I was very nervous and wondered if I would be able to study for an HNC course which is taught in pure English. Even though my English had improved I felt this was the biggest challenge. The interview lasted about forty minutes and concentrated on my work experience as well as my academic background.

"We will let you know the outcome sometime this afternoon" one of the interviewers said.

I was not confident that I would be accepted given that my English was very poor but I had assured the interview panel that I was a very keen learner and that I would learn English at the same time as my HNC course. At home Diane and I nervously waited for the phone to ring and finally it did.

"Good news, she said as she put the phone down. You have been admitted to start after the summer holidays. They wanted to start you at the National Certificate level but because of your considerable work experience in office administration, they have agreed to take you at the Higher National Certificate level instead; but from now on you must work very hard because you need to improve your English if you are to succeed".

"I won't let you down" I said as I hugged Diane realising that this was my other dream almost come true.

From that day I embarked on an English learning journey. I often went to the local library with my pocket French-English dictionary to read. I started with children books because they were easier to read and the words in them were simple. I watched the news and tried to understand what they were saying. I spoke to people all the time. However I found Fifers extremely hard to understand. I bet some of them thought I was deaf because I was always asking them to either repeat or speak slowly. Some of the words I heard from my Fife friends were to be seen nowhere in the dictionary. Phrases like "I dinnie ken" and "dinnie dae that lass" used to confuse me because whenever I checked the words in my dictionary, they were not there.

My efforts to learn English were slowly bearing fruit because by the beginning of August, I could communicate better compared to when I had arrived in June. It was now a week before the college started. Diane helped me to find out about the bus and we did some shopping for stationery. I was overexcited by the events. On the first day, I made some packed lunch and Diane dropped me at the bus station. It was a forty minutes journey to the college. To me, it felt like I was attending a University course. I felt so proud to be part of the young people's crowd going to college even though we hardly spoke to each other. I was also grateful to be admitted at the HNC level having just completed secondary five. But I later found out that in Scotland, universities and colleges' admissions take place when pupils are still in their fifth year. In my country it is different; you have to complete the sixth year before applying for a university or college place.

At college I went in to my first class. The experience was great and moving for me because finally my wish had come true after years of sacrifice. But I found it very hard to understand everything because like many Scots, lecturers spoke very fast. Luckily they gave us lots of literature to read and lots of authors to search for at the library. The day was very long and very unusual. I was used to either work or home so going back to student life after three years and in such a new environment felt very strange.

After a week in to my college life, I received a call from one of the college staff. He wanted to check my passport and visa. After checking my visa, he advised me to immediately apply for a student visa because I was on a visitor's one. At home, Diane called the Home Office only to discover that I wasn't allowed to change my visitor's visa to a student visa from within the United Kingdom. I had to leave the country in order to apply for a student visa. The news came as a deep disappointment for me. After years of hard work, I was enjoying my new life and now I was facing going back home where I wasn't sure I would be granted the student visa. Even if I was granted the visa, there was one problem; my friend and I couldn't afford the ticket to bring me back. After some discussion with my sponsor, we decided to speak to my church minister where I regularly attended church. He and his dear wife were very understanding and very kind. They gave me enough money for my return ticket so at least I could go back with the peace of mind knowing that once the embassy granted me my visa, I had money for the ticket. My flight from London was scheduled for 28th August 1997. I wanted to pack half of my belongings because I felt it was a short trip to get my visa and come back but wise Diane advised me to take all my belongings just in case things didn't go to plan. Like me, my family was very disappointed to hear that I was coming back to Kampala for a student visa.

I arrived in Kampala on Friday 29th August 1997. I had to wait until Monday to apply for the student visa. I promised my family to pay them a visit once I sorted out my visa.

On 30th August 1997, I was shocked to hear about the news of Princess Diane's sudden death. I had seen a lot of her in the British media including the TV and newspapers so it was as if I had personally known her. It is amazing how celebrities and public figures in this country become almost part of your daily life due to media coverage that they receive. Friends in Kampala asked me about her because I had just arrived from Britain. It was very sad.

NO VISA

The following Monday I was one of the first people in the queue. At the interview, the immigration officer seemed satisfied with most things except one - there was no evidence of funds.

"When you provide me evidence of funds such as bank statements I shall review your case" the immigration officer said.

Feeling crushed and disappointed, I left to phone my sponsor. However it was not simple; she couldn't provide what I needed because she had hoped that my course would be funded by the government. The embassy couldn't accept that. After weeks of trying to persuade the embassy's personnel to give me a visa, I gave up and my hope of studying in Europe dissolved in front of me. Upset, angry and disappointed I headed back home to Rwanda. It felt very awkward to go back home because I had said farewell to everyone and they all knew that I had gone to Europe for a long time. At home, most of my friends were shocked to see me back.

"You don't go to Europe especially to Britain and come back" most of them said.

They felt that I had thrown away a golden opportunity and most of them made me feel very stupid.

After a few days, I went to see my ex boss at GTZ where I had resigned in order to go to Britain. He was equally surprised to see me. I explained what had happened about the student visa. I then asked him about the possibility of getting my job back and he agreed to take me back immediately. It was great to have my job back. I kept in touch with Diane hoping to achieve my goal of coming to study in Scotland one day. My English had improved very much that I often interpreted for colleagues and friends. Studying was always at the back of my mind but I needed to work.

MEETING PETER

In November 1997, my brother and I went to visit a friend who had lost her father. There were many people. In many parts of Africa where they are mourning the loss of someone, men sit outside and women sit inside so my brother stayed outside and I went inside the house to be with other girls and women. When it was time to leave, I went to tell my brother. When speaking to my brother Emmanuel, he introduced me to the guy who would later marry me. The introduction was quite brief and short. However the following day, we met again at the same place. This time the conversation with my new friend (Peter) was a bit longer. He could not speak Kinyarwanda because he was a Tanzanian who had arrived a couple of months previously. He was employed as a lecturer at the new Institute of Information and Technology. The new institute needed skilled workers and recruited in neighbouring Tanzania and Kenya so there were about a dozen of them. As I got to know him, I started to like him. He was intelligent, shy and handsome with the manners of a gentleman. He was happy to hear that I was in Britain for a while and asked me more about life in Britain. Even though he had travelled before in Africa and Asia, he hadn't been to Europe or North America. It was his dream to go to America or Europe. That night, he and his friend Matthew escorted us back home; my brother and I invited them to come and meet our family. Soon after that Peter and I became good friends exchanging cards, books, music etc. At Christmas time a special card arrived. Even though I had developed strong feelings for Peter, I wasn't sure he felt the same. As a girl I couldn't tell him how

I felt about him. It would have been strange for it to come from me first so for a date to happen, the request had to come from him first or else there was no chance of us getting any closer. The words on the card however confirmed my wishes. The card was carefully selected and to this day I have never seen such a card. It spoke of love, trust and friendship. From the moment it arrived over the next few days, I read it again and again trying to understand its meaning and relating it to how he felt about me. He was away to Tanzania for Christmas and New Year so I couldn't see him. I impatiently waited his return in order to try and dig more out of him. But he was very shy and didn't give much away so it was going to be a long journey.

When he came back, I'd hoped that he would ask me out but weeks went by without that happening. Each time we met we would have a good conversation but no request for a date with me. However, he kept sending me gifts and cards. The words on the cards spoke of love and romantic feelings but I wanted these words to come from him. The more I spoke to Peter and received cards and gifts from him, the more I fell in love with him but there was not much I could do except wait. After months of friendship, I decided to make the first move and invited him for a meal. He agreed and we went to the golf course restaurant. That afternoon the weather was sunny and the scenery around the course was very beautiful. I only knew about the place because of my muzungu (white) friends otherwise I don't think I would have known about it. It's the type of place where you only saw muzungus and rich people so I had to save some money to afford the outing. At the golf course we sat outside and enjoyed our drinks and brochettes (kebab type). After our meal, we decided to go for a walk in the green wooded countryside beside the course. It was very beautiful. After a few yards into our walk, Peter decided to hold my hand. At this point feelings of love were flowing inside me like electric waves. As we walked, we came across a beautiful small river of water softly flowing in the forest. It was quit and the birds were singing. There was a small bridge with thick concrete blocks so we decided to sit on the concrete blocks and watch the river. We then started to talk about our personal plans. We talked and talked and talked....then a question that led to the conversation which would change my life came.

"What would you like to do?" Peter asked

According to what was going on inside me that time, the answer would have been "I want to be your girlfriend because I'm deeply in love with you" but I couldn't say such things without him expressing his feelings first so I settled with my ancient wish and plan to study. He wanted to know more about why studying meant so much to me; so we talked about the subject for quite a long time. He was quite clearly impressed by my strong desire to go back to study. After that it was my turn to ask him what he wanted to do.

"What do you want to do in life?" I asked.

At this question, he took both my hands and held them whilst looking at me with such eyes filled with love and passion. After a few seconds of silence he said:

"I want to marry you; I want you to become my life partner because I love you very much. From the moment I first met you to this present moment, my love for you keeps growing and now would you be my life partner?"

Then there was an unusual silence, I think because we were both overwhelmed by what was going on inside us. Even though I had been looking forward to the day when I would hear Peter express his love for me, suddenly I felt very scared as strong words from my father who had always strictly warned me about romantic affairs echoed in my mind. And then I opened my mouth to speak and said

"I love you very much too but you are asking me a big question which is to become your life partner. I need time to think about whether I'm ready to commit myself to you for the rest of my life so please give me time and I shall let you know."

"You take as long as you want and I will be here waiting for you" he said as we hugged and passionately kissed for the first time. It was the kiss that I will never forget; he was so good at it that I thought he must have lived in Europe. In Africa we tend to think that men from Europe are more romantic but how wrong!

At home I couldn't sleep for days thinking what decision to make. I knew that I was really in love with Peter but did I really want to get married at that young age? What about my plan to study? Even though he seemed interested, what if he changed his mind and refused to allow me further study? What about my parents? Would they accept marrying their daughter to a foreigner? What about my estranged first boyfriend?

In his last letter, my first boyfriend Oscar made his plan to marry me very clear. He was about to complete his degree course in psychology; his plan was to join me for arrangements of marriage. We had been separated since my family and I moved to Rwanda from Congo in 1994. It was now three years since I'd last seen him and my feelings for him had diminished even thought I still loved him. He kept more in touch with me than I did with him. He never gave up, writing almost every month, sending me tapes of his voice reciting poems of love to me with soft love music in the background. As memories of the good times we had together filled my mind, my love for him started to resurrect. My love was now almost split in two. However, my love for Peter was much stronger. After days and nights of debate in my mind, I felt that it was the right thing to marry Peter. After all, I loved him dearly plus he was mature and able to provide for a wife and family. In Africa, girls are brought up to be dependent on their husbands so it is vital to marry someone who is capable of providing for the family.

I invited him for a meal again. At the restaurant, I found smart Peter waiting. We ordered drinks and meals. I was nervous and avoided bringing up the conversation about love and marriage but after our meals, I had no choice but to tell him my decision.

"I have searched my soul and discovered that I love you too much not to marry you. However there are issues that we need to discuss before deciding to marry each other. I love honesty and as far as marriage is concerned, it is best that I get to know your background and you get to know mine. I will briefly tell you who I am, my family and background and then my future plans".

Naturally I talk a lot and am quite open so within a few minutes I had filled him with my story and background. He looked fascinated as we talked but his fascination turned into shock when I revealed that I had a boyfriend and was not a virgin. I knew that virginity means a lot to African men and that is why I decided to tell him about it rather than let him find out after we'd been together. But as soon as I told him, the look on his face changed. I could see he wasn't happy. He pressed more questions about my past love and I told him as much as I could. Because the atmosphere had changed, I decided it was time to leave. As we walked towards the taxi rank to catch a taxi home, it was my turn to ask Peter about his past love.

"Have you been in love before?" I asked

"No, I have never been in love before".

"Have you ever slept with a woman before? I asked.

"No, never"

"Are you saying that all your life you have never been with a woman?" I asked again

"I have never been with a woman except a girl that I loved but she went to Canada before anything could happen between me and her" he replied.

Surprised and shocked I asked;

"Where have you been all this time to have never had a girlfriend?"

"I have been very busy with my studies plus I joined the army during my gap year between secondary and university. Besides, I became a born again Christian shortly after starting university and was waiting for God to send me a wife."

I didn't know what to think of Peter after learning that he was still a virgin at twenty six. Even though I found it quite strange and almost hard to believe, I thought of him as a saint. I felt awkward to be marrying a virgin when I was not one. He needed another virgin but I loved him very much that I couldn't bear the thought of losing him. The following day I received a nasty letter from him. In it, he'd described me as a prostitute because I was not a virgin as he'd hoped. He even went as far as quoting some scripture in the bible to condemn me. After reading his letter, not only did I feel upset and angry but humiliated as well. I wanted to write a strong nasty letter too but my love for him was great. I couldn't risk losing him so I wrote him a decent one instead. I too quoted some scripture in the bible where it says all have sinned including him. I also briefly explained that I was not a prostitute because it wasn't my habit to sleep around. Just because I had lost my virginity to a guy that I was in love with did not mean I was a prostitute.

A few days after our correspondence, he came to visit me at home. During our conversation he genuinely apologised and asked if I still wanted to be his life partner.

"Of course I do, I love you very much you know"

"I love you very much too" he said

We were both desperate to kiss each other but we could not because we were at my parents' house and until now my parents didn't know about our relationship yet. They thought that Peter was just a friend. Our intimate relationship soon flourished but as Christians we knew not to go as far as sleeping together before marriage so our intimacy could only go as far as kissing and caressing. I wanted to tell my family but the fear of their reaction stopped me. I knew that my parents would oppose our relationship because of his nationality. Rwandans are not very keen to marry their daughters to foreigners. I kept delaying breaking the news. They knew about my first boyfriend Oscar who was from Burundi. Even though they had strongly opposed it, they gradually accepted him. Somehow they believed that he was the one who was going to marry me. But after many years apart, they were pleased to see that the relationship was slowly dying meaning that their plan for me to marry a fellow Rwandan or a white guy would succeed. You can imagine their shock when I told them about Peter who was from Tanzania.

OVER MY DEAD BODY

Even though Tanzania is our neighbour, its people are seen as very foreign because of the difference in culture and language. Papa went berserk when I told him that Peter was indeed the guy that I wanted to marry.

"Over my dead body!" he said

"But I love him very much papa."

"From today I want your relationship to end. If I see you with him again, I shall make it my personal business to deal with him."

"That's very unfair, papa. I'm twenty two and I have the right to marry who I want. The legal age is twenty one so I don't see any reason why you should force me to abandon him"

"I'm your father and as far as father-daughter relationship is concerned, you either choose him and lose me or call off you relationship and remain my daughter." papa said loudly.

I couldn't believe what I was hearing. I was being asked the hardest thing to do; choose between the guy I loved with all my heart and papa, whom I dearly loved too but whose dictatorship I didn't like. I hated the culture of arranging marriage for girls and I had decided not to be one of them, so I was ready to fight for my rights but didn't want to lose my beloved papa either. That night I left the sitting room without expressing my decision and for the first time in my life I spent a few days without talking to my beloved papa. I avoided him as much as he avoided me. One night however papa got drunk in order to confront me on the issue. This time I felt I had to obey him so I promised him to stop seeing Peter.

The following day, I went round to Peter's house in order to tell him that we couldn't carry on seeing each other because the family had strongly opposed our relationship. We both agreed that it was a good idea to stop seeing each other. But we soon discovered that we couldn't live without each other. The love between us was strong and burning. I arranged to meet with Peter soon after receiving a miss you card from him. We were both dying to see each other again and we spent a long time together. At home papa had arrived before me. In the past, I had always managed to be home before papa's arrival to avoid annoying him. This time it was different because I found an angry papa waiting for me:

"Where have you been?" he angrily asked.

"I have been to see Peter" I calmly replied.

"How dare you disobey me? I am your father and you must obey my rules. You wait here; I shall deal with you when I come back from Peter's."

"No papa, please don't go round there disturbing him. It's my fault that we have started seeing each other again. Please leave him alone and deal with me" I said with panic.

"I have to warn him not to ever see or touch you again" he replied as he stormed off the house to go to Peter's."

Peter and his friend Matthew lived a few streets from ours. I was not only deeply embarrassed by papa's sudden angry visit to Peter's but was also very scared of what he might do. I couldn't follow him so all I could do was to wait. After a few minutes, he stormed back into the sitting room where mama and I were nervously waiting for him.

"I have told your so called boyfriend that if I ever see you and him together again, I shall kill him" he said.

"Papa, that's unfair because I deeply love him"

After an intensive argument, I left to stay with my cousin who lived in the neighbourhood. I couldn't stand papa's dictatorship even though I knew he meant well. My cousin reassured me that he was acting with my best interests at heart. The following day, my cousin and I went to see Auntie Anne-Marie in order to ask her to speak to papa and persuade him that I was in love and that there wasn't much he could do about it. At home things didn't go as well as I had anticipated. Papa became even more furious at the fact that I had left and came back with other members of the family to speak to him. After a meeting with mama and my auntie, we decided that I should cool the relationship, so from that day I only saw Peter secretly.

PETER IS ACCEPTED

The clandestine relationship between Peter and I went on for months until one day in September 1998 I told papa that Peter was still my friend and that he had offered to sponsor me to study in Britain. We all knew that Peter was wealthy because he worked as an expatriate. Expatriates usually earn very good salaries compared to local ones so both papa and I knew that Peter was capable of paying for my college fees. After questioning his motives and intentions, I explained to papa that we were still madly in love but wouldn't marry before I completed my course in Britain. This was the answer we had been waiting for; to get a sponsor to pay for my college fees since accommodation and other expenses were going to be covered by Diane. Papa is very pro-education so he couldn't resist the offer to educate his daughter abroad. Plus he had seen how strong the love between Peter and I was and had begun trusting him. He agreed to our plans and blessed them. He then decided to invite Peter for a meal in order to get to know him; after all he was now going to be his future son-in-law. One day, papa and Peter went out for a meal. That evening I couldn't be happier; papa and Peter had made up and became good friends. Papa blessed our relationship and any plans that we may have together. What a happy chapter in our relationship. I had missed the start date so we agreed that I should enrol for starting college in September 1999. However my English needed to improve further so in November 1998 I enrolled in a local English speaking boarding school where I went on to do my sixth year. After all these years, it felt very strange to be a pupil again. Despite my poor English, I excelled with the help of extra tuition and hard work. Peter was my main provider. He provided everything from school fees to spending money. I was very lucky to have met a guy who cared so much that he decided to support my education. I thanked God day and night for Peter's generosity and care.

UNPLANNED EVENTS

Our love continued to flourish and I spent most of my holidays going round to visit Peter. Each time we would get physically closer. A few months before the end of my school year and in February 1999 we got too close. I panicked when I missed my period in March. Then I started to feel sick and tired.

"Peter, I think I'm pregnant" I said.

"No way" he replied.

"Well my periods have not started and I'm not feeling well."

"But how?"

"I don't know! The only way to find out is to go to the hospital for a pregnancy test."

"Right, here is the money. Please call me once you come from the hospital."

"Ok!" I said.

That night, I couldn't sleep. I spent the whole night planning my next move.

"If I'm pregnant, what am I going to do? What if Peter doesn't want anything to do with the baby?" I thought.

Even though I greatly feared family, friends and fellow Christians' reactions at the news that I was pregnant before marriage, I decided from that night that if I was pregnant, I would keep my precious baby.

The following day, I secretly went to a private hospital for a pregnancy test. The doctor scanned me and said "you are six weeks pregnant."

Although I suspected my pregnancy, nothing could have prepared me for the news. For a family like mine which believed in proper ways to behave and live, getting pregnant before marriage was not acceptable. However, I felt great responsibility and great love for my baby and decided to face the critics and concentrate on its best interests.

After the confirmation of my pregnancy, I went to the hospital's toilet, knelt down and said a special prayer for my precious unborn baby. I loved it very much that I prayed for its protection as I didn't want my baby to suffer from the stigma attached to children born before or outside marriage. I also prayed that Peter would take the news well. I then rang Peter and asked to meet with him. He too was shocked at the news and couldn't say much. He questioned if the pregnancy was his and I furiously said that it was his. I couldn't believe the cheek!

"Look, if you are prepared to accept me and the child then we better hurry up and arrange the wedding before this pregnancy is big. If you are not prepared to marry me, please let me know your intentions as soon as possible so that I can make other plans." I said.

"I will think about it and I shall let you know my intentions as soon as possible."

As I lay that night, I felt great responsibility since I wasn't sure that Peter would marry me. In Africa men often deny pregnancies and leave women and girls to carry full responsibility without playing any part in the child's upbringing. Countless children live without knowing their fathers due to this common practice.

Thoughts went through my mind like a crazy woman,

What will I do if Peter doesn't want to be involved in this child's life?

What will happen to my education abroad?

What about my family and friends? Will they ever speak to me again? They will all probably disown me?

Nobody will ever want to know me again? They will all run away when they see me; I know they will.

Oh please God, let Peter accept me and marry me because I can't stand facing people if he doesn't.

If he doesn't marry me then I shall run away. I shall go to start a new life somewhere because I can't bear staying where everyone will look at me and think of me so lowly. Plus I don't want to bring my child up in an environment where he will be seen and treated as illegitimate.

I shall leave this place and go away - yes I will.

I couldn't help but panic about what was going to happen to me and my precious unborn child. The following day Peter arranged for us to meet and I was very relieved to hear that he was going to marry me. He was quite reluctant but felt great responsibility for his unborn child. Without delaying, we decided to marry in May. The problem would be to persuade papa and mama about a wedding before the completion of my school year. I couldn't tell them the truth because they would take it so badly. So I had to make up a plan that would persuade my parents to let us marry soon.

That night I started what seemed to be the hardest conversation I have ever had with my parents. Usually I went to bed before my parents but this time I was hanging around with papa and mama far later than my usual bed time not knowing what to say. Then papa asked me:

"Are you not going to bed?"

"Not now because I have something to tell you"

"Peter and I have been doing a lot of talking. As you know I'm hoping to go to Britain this year for my further studies. Diane was on the phone to Peter last week and has confirmed my admission with Glenrothes College. I'm hoping to start an HNC[3] course in Business Administration in August this year"

"Very good!" papa said

"But Peter and I have decided to marry before I go because he's planning to join me there and he can't come to live with me if we aren't married"

"Are you saying that you want to marry this year?" mama asked looking surprised, because we had previously agreed that I would marry after my course in Scotland.

"Yes, because if he's planning to join me in Scotland, then it's best that we marry sooner rather than later".

"So when are you planning to marry?" papa asked

"22nd of May" I said looking rather unsure that they would accept this kind of very short notice.

"How can we prepare for a wedding in only two months? Besides we are not in the financial position to organise a wedding for you because we need time to save. You know how costly weddings are, don't you?" papa said

"Don't worry about the financial side of it because Peter has agreed to help. He will meet some of the expenses such as my dress, shoes and other things"

"Even so, we still need time to notify your extended family in villages" papa said, with a look that suggested they were strongly against this quick wedding.

"But papa, it is what we both want" I said looking desperate to persuade them.

"Why are you rushing things?" mama asked

"Well, because I want to go to Scotland knowing that we are both committed to each other".

"Okay, we need to speak to the rest of the family and see what they think" papa said.

"Does that mean it is ok with you two?"

"Well if that's what you want, yeah it is fine with us."

I was very happy to see that both my parents had agreed with our plans. I knew that the rest of the family wouldn't say no if papa and mama were for the wedding.

WEDDING

Preparations for the wedding began. A wedding in my country is a big deal; it's almost like organising a royal visit. There are four big separate ceremonies. Each one is followed by a reception. It costs a lot, but luckily money was not a big issue because my soon-to-be husband had money. However my family had to contribute towards the costs so they got friends and family together to raise funds. Money raised was going to be used at one of the ceremonies which is organised by the bride's family. We had just over two months to prepare for the big day. I wanted the best wedding ever. With one hundred and fifty invitations distributed, we had to plan for at least two hundred and fifty people because in Africa invited people don't come on their own; they usually bring their whole family and friends with them. Even though I had the help of friends and family, I wanted to make sure that everything went according to my plan. Therefore I had to leave school in order to concentrate on the organisation of my wedding. Part of the preparations that I most enjoyed was looking for my wedding dress. I loved trying all sort of dresses. Some of them made me look like Cinderella and some made me look like a real princess. Finally I settled down with a long sleeved white dress with the top filled with tiny beautiful shiny beads. Peter trusted me and left me in charge of everything. But it wasn't easy because I was a few weeks pregnant and therefore felt very tired.

After weeks of preparations, the week of the wedding arrived. Most members of my extended family lived outside Kigali so they started to arrive a few days before the wedding day. The party began a week before the actual wedding. By Wednesday, we had more than thirty people in our three bedroom house. Somehow we all managed to sleep comfortably. Some slept in the bedrooms and some slept in the living room. We even had people sleeping in the corridor. The atmosphere was great. I was the star of the week and everyone wanted to speak to me. I was enjoying the attention I received from friends and family.

I had hoped that a few members of Peter's family would attend the wedding from Tanzania but I soon learned that only his cousin was going to come. He would arrive on Friday night just in time for the following day's event.

THURSDAY 20TH MAY 1999

It's the first ceremony and an important one because without it your marriage is invalid in the eyes of the law. It's the civil one and will take place at the commune office (Registrar) at three o' clock. With my beautiful prêt a porter skirt and jacket ready, I head off to the best hairdresser in the city. Somehow I'm a lot calmer than I thought I would be. My hair done, I go back home and find out that I'm the only person not dressed for the occasion. People are so excited that they have put on their best outfits a few hours before. It's two o' clock and Peter could be here anytime to collect me. Transport for friends and family has been organised. I don't know which car I will be in because Peter and his friends were in charge of organising for the groom and bride's transport. Now I start to get a little bit nervous. I can't eat so I drink lot of milk instead, which isn't helpful to my already active bladder but I need energy. As my matron of honour puts the finishing touches to my make-up, my sister comes running. "Baraje" she shouts which means "they're coming." We have hired a video man and a photographer so the filming starts immediately when Peter and his friends enter the gates. After the greetings, Peter holds my hand and we walk towards the posh, well decorated 4X4 jeep which is waiting outside on the non-tarmac road.

At the registrar there are about eight couples so the ceremony is going to take longer. After the civil wedding, we head to Pane Vine restaurant where we had booked a small reception for thirty people. After drinking and eating brochettes, people talk, laugh and rejoice.

After an hour at the reception, it's time to go home and prepare for the big day. I kiss Peter good bye.

FRIDAY 21ST MAY 1999

I spend Friday chatting to my family and friends. It's like a hen day. As usual in our tradition, aunties fill me with all sorts of advice on how to be a good wife. Some limit their advice to housework and submission as a wife but others go as far as explaining sex life in marriage.

"You must make it your priority to satisfy your husband's sexual needs" one of my aunties says.

Another one adds "it will be painful when you aren't up to it but you mustn't complain."

It scares me to see that none of their advices includes my rights as a wife. It's all about my responsibilities. I go to my bed at around one o' clock in the morning but I find it hard to sleep. This is my last day as a single girl. I'm now going to be a wife and a mother. I'm excited and yet scared at the same time, especially after my aunties' advice. I feel like I'm setting myself a trap by going into a marriage which sounds like a prison where I have to do what the husband says. Having such an independent mind makes it very hard for me to understand how on earth I would be a submissive wife. I don't mind discussing issues with my husband and reaching for solutions together but I don't expect him to treat me like a second class person who must do his will, something very common in Africa. I witnessed and still witness many marriages where wives don't have much say in how their family is run and I had vowed not to allow the same to happen to me. That's why I want to be educated in order not to depend on my husband for every single penny that I would need. Often women are stuck in situations where they have no choice because they can not support themselves. I don't want this to be the case with me. Even though I worry about these things, it doesn't stop the excitement that I feel because so far Peter doesn't present himself as one of those men anyway. So there is reason for me to have peace. As I lay in bed, I also imagine my new home and how I'm now going to live with Peter whom I deeply love. No more time limits in our relationship, no more feelings of missing him, from now on we shall be together and enjoy life together. I'm also looking forward to staying in a villa with everything. There is a television, fridge etc. But I feel that I shall miss living with papa and mama very much. I shall miss their guidance, the sense of security and papa's strictness. Finally I fall asleep very late into the night.

SATURDAY 22ND MAY 1999

The first ceremony of the day is "Gusaba no Gukwa", the official demand for my hand and the payment of a dowry price. It's expected to take place at ten in the morning. My family and friends have prepared and decorated the hall where we shall welcome Peter and his family when they come. Papa is not allowed to speak at the ceremony so he asked his best pal Mr Paul Mugisha to speak on behalf of our family. Peter and his family will need a speaker too. Sitting arrangement is such that Peter's family sit on one side facing my family. Marriage in my country used to be arranged by two families. In those days, the groom and the bride didn't know each other until the wedding day. These traditions are now carried out in a modern way because the bride and groom know each other before. Although Peter will be there, I will not be allowed in the hall until the dowry price has been paid.

At seven in the morning a taxi takes me along with my matron of honour Francoise to the hairdresser. Long extensions had already been fixed to my hair the previous day. After trying on both tiaras on which I brought with me, the hairdresser has an idea of what hair style would suit both of them. I'm under the dryer when I see my brother Emmanuel standing in front of me. Since I don't expect him there, I get out from under the dryer to ask him what he's doing in the salon.

"I'm afraid to say that I have some bad news" he said.

My matron, who came out from under her dryer to listen to our conversation, pulls my brother away rushing him to the corner, in order to avoid worrying or stressing me on my wedding day, but it's too late because at this point my heart is beating fast thinking what could be the bad news. So I rush after them saying to Francoise that it's ok and that I'm ready for any news.

"Due to some problems, the dance group can't perform at tonight's reception" Emmanuel said.

"Oh no, this is very bad! What are we going to do?" I said in a panic

A wedding reception without the traditional dancing group to entertain guests is not a proper one. Luckily we happen to know someone who is in charge of another traditional dancing group. With no phone facility to ring her friend, Francoise asks my brother to go and see her. A couple of hours later, we are relieved to hear that the group will perform at tonight's reception.

It's nine o' clock and we have come back home from the salon. Papa works for the institute of agriculture and husbandry. His post qualified him for one of the institute's properties so we stay in the institute's complex which has residences, offices and a hall. The hall where the ceremony will be taking place is just yards from our house so it makes it easier for us to watch guests coming from our bedroom window.

By nine forty five, most people are seated in the hall waiting to welcome Peter and his family. They arrive on time, something unusual in African weddings. Everyone is looking forward to this ceremony because it is hilarious how the bride's family teases the groom's family.

After welcoming the guests, the master of ceremony introduces the two speakers and the much awaited dialogue between the two of them begins.

"What reason has brought you here today that you have brought so many people with you?" my family's speaker asks.

"We have come to ask for the hand of one of your daughters because one of my sons has fallen in love with her."

"Well, I have many daughters and it would be very difficult for me to guess who you are after, because they are all beautiful and most of them are ready to be married."

"My son fell in love with Chantal."

"Who is your son?"

"Come on son! stand up so that everyone can see you."

Embarrassed, Peter then stands up to a round of applause.

"That is my son, Peter; he is handsome, mature and capable of looking after your daughter, Chantal."

"I can see that. However there is one problem, Chantal went to visit her aunty in another province and is not here for us to check with her if this is truly the guy with whom she fell in love, so I am afraid to say that you'll have to come back another day."

"But that is impossible because Chantal knew that we were coming here today; knowing how much she loves my son, I'm sure she would not miss it for the world; maybe she is back from visiting her aunty but because we are all here in the hall, you are probably not aware that she is at home, so please send one of her brothers to see if she is back."

At this point one of the guests shouted "I'm Chantal's brother; I'm late but I came with Chantal and she's at home"

Everyone laughs and claps their hands to see that this carry on between the two speakers is cut short by confirming that indeed I'm at home.

"Honourable friend, now that it has been confirmed that Chantal is here, I would like to ask for her hand" Peter's speaker said.

"Chantal belongs to a big family so I need to ask the whole family if they are prepared to marry our daughter to your son. Therefore I'm asking you to come another day."

"I understand what you are saying but we are very lucky to have most of Chantal's family here today so it is my wish that you ask them now so that we can move on to the next stage."

"Right, give me a few minutes" my family's speaker said.

He then turned to everyone on my family's side to ask them if they are happy to marry me to Peter. Everyone is happy with this idea except two guys who refuse to accept to marry me to Peter because of the things that Peter's family had done to them (these reasons are made up in order to reflect how it used to work a long time ago).

After sincere apologies from Peter's family, our speaker finally agrees to give my hand by saying:

"We have known you & your family and have been good friends for a long time. It will be wrong of me not to let you have Chantal who is in love with your son Peter. Please look after her and remember that her name means don't make her cry so make sure you don't upset her."

Guests are delighted to see that I'm traditionally allowed to marry Peter and everyone claps their hands.

"I thank you very much for giving me the hand of Chantal. She will be one of my children. She shall lack nothing nor will she suffer or be upset. Please accept this hoe as a token of my gratitude. I also have a field full of cows and it is my duty and pleasure to give you some of them as a dowry price."

After discussions, the two parties agree the dowry price of two big cows. Peter's speaker then hands an envelope to my family's speaker. In it is a cheque equivalent to the current price of two big cows.

Traditionally, real cows should be given and in rural areas where people have farms, they still give cows but in cities where people don't have farms, money is given instead.

Everybody is happy that a deal has been made and after paying the dowry price, Peter's family want to see me so someone comes to get me together with my five bridesmaids. We are all dressed in our traditional outfits. I look beautiful but am very nervous.

In the hall everybody claps their hands when they see us. It's so good to see so many friends and family gathered together for my special day. There must be more than one hundred people at the ceremony. I exchange gifts with my fiancé. This is also known as our engagement. I was surprised to see that engagement in the west is very simple - just by popping the question "would you marry me?"; in my country engagement takes place in a big ceremony where the family of the girl officially accepts the boy to marry their daughter and the boy's family pays the dowry price.

We are then entertained by my Christians friends who perform very well and the ceremony comes to an end at about twelve fifteen in the afternoon.

The church ceremony is expected at two o' clock followed by a reception at five o' clock. We don't have much time left so as Peter and his family leave, we rush back home to start getting ready for the biggest event of the day.

Somehow I'm full of energy even though I'm pregnant and haven't been eating well. At home mama and my aunties force me to eat something. By one thirty, I'm dressed in my wedding gown and am ready to marry Peter. With the full make up and the tiara on my head, I look stunning. People can't stop staring at me and they keep saying that I look like a real queen and I feel like a real queen too. We have a family photographer who takes lots of photos. Papa and mama look very proud to be marrying their daughter in what can only be described as a lavish ceremony - well, compared to other weddings of people of my background, it is lavish.

We are all ready and are waiting for the groom to come. Unlike here, back home the groom is driven in the wedding car to the bride's house to collect her and they both go to the church together. It's two thirty and the groom hasn't appeared. We are running very late and I start to wonder whether Peter has changed his mind and isn't coming at all. In the past, I'd heard stories where either the groom or bride didn't turn up on their wedding day. But the fact he was present at both the civil and traditional ceremonies means surely he is up to it. I'm relieved to see a handsome and very smart Peter arrive with his best man and page boy. From the house to the place where our car is parked, we walk hand in hand accompanied by happy friends and family singing to us. After a lot of manoeuvring to get my long, wide wedding dress properly in the car, we're comfortably seated inside the well decorated Mercedes Benz estate car. I'm so pleased to see that we are being followed by a cortege of more than fifteen cars. In the car I can't help but cry with joy so before going inside the church my matron of honour gives me a quick make-up and pleads with me not to cry again. We arrive at three o' clock and the service immediately starts as we are very late. The church is packed and I can't believe all these smartly dressed people have gathered to see Peter and I get married. I'm honoured to see that so many people have turned up. The service finishes at five thirty and we head to the famous city garden for photographs. At six o' clock we are at the hall where the reception is taking place. Everyone is in the hall except the bride, groom and their helpers. We then walk in to a huge round of applause by guests. They all stand to honour us. The whole experience humbles me as I feel greatly privileged to be the star of the day. There must be more than two hundred people. We sit at the high table. After the initial speeches by the master of ceremony, entertainment starts followed by drinks and food. Our friend's four daughters also give us a surprise entertainment by singing and dancing. The songs are hilarious in particular the one which says:

"Brother Peter, we love you very much
We went to the garden to get you some flowers and couldn't get any
But don't worry because you have now got Chantal"

It's the end of the wedding reception. I'm very pleased and relieved to see that everything has gone very well. We then head to my new home at about eight thirty in the evening. For the first time, Peter and I get to spend some time alone in our bedroom which has been well prepared for the newly married couple. It feels so good to fall in his arms with relief that I'm finally his wife. We are both very excited and over the moon to be together. Lost in our love world, we forget that there is yet another ceremony to follow. Someone knocks on our bedroom door to remind us to get ready for the next and final ceremony which will start at ten o' clock. It has been such a long day and I honestly don't feel like leaving Peter. But I don't have any choice because this next traditional ceremony is very important too. It's called "gutwikurura" which means to unveil. In olden days newly married brides stayed inside the house for a period of at least one to three months. At the end of this period the bride's aunties came to her room and officially brought her outside. In modern days no bride can stay inside the house for such a long period, so the ceremony is done either on the same day, if you're going for honeymoon the following day, or in a week's time for those not going anywhere for honeymoon. We had our honeymoon booked in Gisenyi, northern Rwanda, so the ceremony has to take place the same day.

By ten o' clock, we've both changed into our outfits waiting for my aunties. They, together with friends come with so much food and gifts for my new home. Gifts include food, toiletries, household utensils etc.

The gifts are packed in traditionally made baskets known as "ibiseke". These ibiseke are carried by young ladies who form a queue and walk into the house leaving the baskets in the kitchen. My aunties then come into the bedroom where Peter and I are waiting covered by a veil. One of my aunties unveils us reciting words of blessings to the new couple. Another aunty cuts a little bit of my hair to declare me a married woman. In olden days girls had a specific hair style known as "amasunzu". Once they became married they had to get rid of the style by cutting their amasunzu into a normal plain style. After the cutting of my hair, we are given milk in a wooden jar. We both drink it and then we both feed the milk to two toddlers signifying prosperity and children.

We then go to the marquee outside where people have gathered to enjoy more drink, food and chatting. It's almost midnight and I have little energy left. I can't wait for people to leave. When the master of ceremony stands up, I breathe a sigh of relief convinced that he's going to give closing remarks but I soon discover that he's giving Peter's cousin a chance to speak on behalf of their family whose many members couldn't make it to the wedding. Some of my friends also decide to sing and another guy gives another speech. There must have been one hundred speeches today and I have lost track of speakers. Finally the closing remarks come at about one o' clock in the morning and as people hug me to say farewell, it suddenly dawns on me that I'm no longer a single girl but a married woman. Another eventful day has come to an end and the beginning of a new chapter of my life has just started. I kiss and hug my sisters, brothers, aunties, cousins and friends with a flood of tears rolling down my cheeks. Even though I miss my dearest family already but it feels wonderful to be besides Peter.

HONEYMOON

The following day we head to Gisenyi for a week's holiday. What a honeymoon! The best! Gisenyi is very beautiful and our hotel's windows overlook the Lake Kivu. The hotel has its private beach area so we often dine there. After a week, we go back home to prepare for another couple of ceremonies. The next ceremony is known as "**guca kw'irembo**" which means to pass through the gates. It takes place a week after the wedding. Peter and I have to visit my family. We have to take drinks with us and there will be speakers to mark the ceremony. The following week my parents and family have to come and visit us. They too have to bring food and drinks. I'm very relieved and happy to see that all these ceremonies go well and oh boy! I'm so pleased to see that they are finally over.

Peter goes back to work and I enjoy being a housewife. There are two girls who help with the housework which means I always enjoy a long lie in the mornings and I relax as much as possible. Nothing feels better than being a housewife to not only a good looking guy but who is quite well off. We even have a car and a chauffeur. He drives me wherever and whenever I want to go. I often visit mama because she too is a housewife so we hang about together doing shopping and catching up. After a month people start to notice that my belly is bigger than usual so they start pressing questions. I do my best to avoid such conversations by moving on to other subjects. Meantime my plans to travel to Britain, which were once approved without any problem, are now under negotiation since Peter seems to have changed his mind.

SECOND TRIP TO SCOTLAND

TANZANIA

After a few months of negotiations, Peter finally agreed to let me travel to Scotland for my further studies but we both agreed that it was best I first visited his family and then travelled to Scotland from Tanzania. We originally planned travelling to Tanzania together in August but due to work he couldn't get his holidays so I had to be brave and go to meet my new

in-laws alone. Luckily one of my brothers-in-law was at the wedding, so at least there was going to be a familiar face.

Before leaving, I told mama that I was a few months pregnant and she was quite shocked because it was too soon.

"But surely you can't go now that you're pregnant" she said with her face displaying worry.

"I will be fine mama; I can't throw this chance away." I replied.

"What about the baby? How are going to study in a far away land with a young baby and without your family to help you?"

"Peter will probably join me sooner rather than later; plus Diana my sponsor will help" I reassured her.

However I wasn't sure if this latter statement was true because Diana didn't know I was pregnant.

After reassuring her, she reluctantly accepted the trip.

Only three moths after my magical wedding, I had to leave my husband and family in order to travel first to his country and then to

Britain. The plan was to apply for a student visa in Dar es Salaam, the capital city of Tanzania as the British embassy in Rwanda didn't deal with issuing visas. Peter and my family accompanied me to the airport. It was very emotional to leave my family and Peter behind. I cried all the way to Dar es Salaam, Tanzania.

There were half a dozen people from Peter's family who had come to collect me from the airport. I didn't know what to expect of them nor did I know what they expected of me. When I first met them, I was shy but as an outgoing person I couldn't help but be myself. Luckily we seemed to be getting on very well and within a few days, I was just like another daughter in the house. I loved Peter's mother. She was a cool, calm and very intelligent lady. She wasn't like the normal African ladies of her age who are often stuck in cultivating fields and looking after many children. She was well educated and a college lecturer who has had only two children. She was very modern and a no nonsense lady. Her house was always kept tidy. Although she had a house helper, she preferred to wake up early in the morning in order to make chapatti (pancakes) for us before going to work. She trusted her own cooking better than that of the house girl. I admired this lady and I felt so proud to be her daughter-in-law. I loved Peter's granny too who upon my arrival, came to meet me with flowers in her hands, but then jokingly said that I was now her rival since I had married her husband. In some parts of Africa, grandsons pretend to be their grannies' husbands and granddaughters pretend to be their grandpas' wives. I spent weeks with the family getting to know them. Peter then joined me in September for a few days. While in Tanzania, we seized the opportunity for me to apply for the student visa. Even though like mama, my mother-in-law wasn't keen for me to travel and study abroad while pregnant, Peter and I still went ahead with the plan.

That morning, after handing all documents and evidence of funds to the visa officer, he asked me to return at two o' clock in the afternoon. Upon my return I was handed my passport and was extremely pleased to see that I had been granted a student visa for one year. It meant my dream of studying was now going to come true.

HEATHROW

I had already missed the college start date so there was not much time. The earliest flight to London was in a week's time. The week gave me time to prepare myself and say farewell.

It was 10th September and the day before my departure. I visited a private clinic to ensure that my health and pregnancy were fine. I got the all clear from the doctor. I kept the scan picture with me in case it was needed where I was going. That night Peter and I couldn't sleep. It was very hard to imagine life in a far away land without him or our families. But I was excited at the same time at the idea of coming to study in Europe.

On 11th September, many of my in-laws accompanied me to the airport. After saying the emotional farewell, I boarded the huge Gulf Air plane on the way to London via Muscat. By now, I was somehow getting used to flying. Looking back into my childhood, I couldn't understand how I had reached this point. If there was anything that felt so sweet in the entire world, it was the experience of coming from extreme poverty to having it all.

After almost fifteen hours of travelling including the transit, we were finally at Heathrow airport on 12th September at five o' clock in the morning. At the immigration desk there was a long queue. One of the immigration officers walking around started to randomly call some of the passengers in the queue aside. I was one of those picked by him. There must have been half a dozen of us when he took us to his office where we were asked to wait. He checked the first few who were before me. The lady besides me panicked a lot because she had a fake visa and didn't have genuine contacts in Britain. She asked me if I could pass on my sponsor's details to her so that she can pass them to the officer as her contact. I categorically said no because how on earth was I going to explain to Diane my sponsor who this young lady was? I had just met her there. Besides, Diane didn't know her at all.

It was now my turn to go to the interview room. The officer asked me a few questions and seemed satisfied. However his satisfaction turned into doubts when he checked my luggage and discovered the pregnancy scan picture. Suddenly the look on his face and his tone changed. The much respect and gentleness that he seemed to have shown me when he knew that I was simply a student disappeared.

"Are you pregnant?" he asked looking rather surprised, as he hadn't noticed anything since I was wearing a large West African dress.

"Yes, sir."

"How many weeks?"

"I'm expecting to give birth on 30th October."

"How are you going to study when you have a baby to care for?"

"Diane is going to help me and when she is not able to do so, the baby will be at the crèche. I also have many other friends whom I'm sure will be happy to help."

"We want to be sure that your baby will be in good care when you're studying. I need to speak to Diane to confirm what you have just said to me. If she agrees to help with the care of your child then I will allow you entry, if not then I am afraid I have to send you back."

I gave the officer the telephone number. As I waited for him to come through I could not help but panic. I have never panicked so much in my life before. After such a long trip and after such hard work to convince my family and husband to let me come, the last thing I needed was what I was hearing. Plus Diane didn't have a clue that I was pregnant so I thought *"this call will freak her and she will just say no to the immigration officer's question about the care of my baby and then I will be sent back home."*

I hated the thought of being sent home again. Luckily there was good news.

"Good news" he said as he opened the door to take his seat.

"Diane has confirmed that childcare arrangements can be made. You are now free to go but I need you to be checked by the airport doctor just to ensure that you and your baby are both well. Meantime would you like a cup of tea?"

This guy suddenly turned very nice because my God-sent angel, sponsor Diane had confirmed that I was genuine and that everything was under control. Only God knows how much I will be ever grateful to Diane who rescued me on that day. After the health checks, I was allowed entry. I immediately phoned Diane who understandably expressed her shock to hear that I was pregnant.

SCOTLAND

My bus to Scotland was at night time so I had the whole day to explore London. I left my luggage at Victoria station where my bus to Scotland was going to depart from and went to see London. It was fascinating to see the tall buildings and busyness of the city. I kept thinking London is really what I had imagined it to be - lots of cars and underground trains; lots of people walking fast and lots of shops and offices etc. After such a hectic day, I was finally in my bus heading for Scotland. We arrived the following morning at about eight o' clock. Diane collected me from the bus station which is about twenty minutes away from her place.

After the initial excitements of seeing each other,

"Why didn't you tell me that you are pregnant?"

"I was scared that you wouldn't sponsor me."

"You are right. I wouldn't have sponsored you if I knew you were pregnant."

This statement from Diane made me feel better that I had made the right decision not to mention anything about my pregnancy to her until I saw her.

"What are you going to do? How will you study when you have the baby?"

"I will find a solution. Surely there are crèches here."

"Yeah, but they are very expensive"

"Don't worry Diane, I will sort the childcare issue, I assure you that you won't have to look after my baby."

"What about accommodation? You know this place will be small once the baby is here".

"I will sort that one too," I reassured worried Diane.

"You are very welcome to stay here as long as you want, but long term it will be best for you to get a flat"

"Yeah, you are very right, Diane, because Peter is going to join me at some point, so I will definitely need a place of my own sooner rather than later."

I loved the honesty in Diane. She tackled the issues directly and was always honest about her feelings, which is unlike where I come from. In Africa, people would rather die than express their concerns to their guests.

She advised me to register with the local General Practitioner (GP) so that I could start attending antenatal clinics.

Within days of registering, I was allocated a mid wife and attended the antenatal clinic regularly. I was amazed at the extent of care provided to pregnant women in this country. In Africa, for people who can afford it, you have to pay for each visit you make to the antenatal clinic. Very few pregnant women attend antenatal clinics unless there is something wrong with them or their pregnancies.

I went back to my church. Members of the church were very pleased to see me after more than two years. The minister and his family who had helped me in 1997 were equally happy to see me. On my first visit, they invited me for lunch and since that day it has become a tradition to go to my minister's house for lunch after the Sunday service. I can count how many Sundays we haven't shared lunch or indeed dinner with my generous kind hearted minister and his family. They became very much involved in helping me settle in this country. I was very fortunate to have genuine friends such as Diane, John and the Doyle family to help me.

I started college as soon as I arrived and was enjoying learning. I found it hard to begin with, because I was quite heavily pregnant and I loved the fact that I was back to college without any problems. Without any problems? Well, so I had imagined until I discovered how much fees the college was going to charge me as a foreign student. I couldn't believe it when the finance officer told me how much I was to pay. It was thousands of pounds because I was a foreigner student. *"How on earth are we going to afford this amount of money?"* I asked myself when I left his office. Even though Peter had agreed to sponsor me, not once had it crossed our minds that college fees would cost this much. Plus, he now needed to help pay for accommodation and child care which all cost a fortune. I wasn't brave enough to ask Diane for financial help as she had already done me a favour by supplying a sponsorship letter to the embassy and helping me settle in this country. I sat down with my pen and paper and calculated how much I needed a month to survive; the budget, which included college fees and childcare expense was well over £1900. This was far beyond our financial ability so another hope to study was under fire. I was very upset and couldn't understand why my dream of studying that I had always wanted throughout my life kept dissolving each time an opportunity would arise. I began to think that maybe it was not my fate or destiny to have a degree. I was quite miserable but I kept attending college anyway with the hope that another miracle would happen.

One day, I had a long telephone conversation with a Rwandan friend who was living in London. In the end, she persuaded me to claim for asylum since I was a Rwandan. She had been successful in doing so and was now towards the end of her degree course. I didn't fancy the idea of claiming asylum and becoming a refugee again after almost a lifetime of just that. However, I had no other option and had nothing to lose. At the college, I browsed the internet and discovered that Rwanda was listed under those countries whose citizens could claim for asylum in the United Kingdom. With only three weeks to go before the arrival of my baby, I went to Edinburgh's Scottish Refugee Council. After quite a long wait at the reception, a case worker finally called me into the interview room. My English had improved but I still found it hard to converse fluently so she asked me if I needed an interpreter. I declined the offer because it was always my belief to help myself. We had hours of chat talking about my experiences as a Tutsi. I had to describe all the events that had affected my family as a result of the ongoing conflict between Hutu rebels and the government. After a very long interview, my case worker advised me to go home and have the baby before we could do anymore. I qualified for help whilst waiting so she gave me a letter to take to Social Work.

Social Work services allocated me a Social worker who would assist me. She was the best social worker I could have wished for. The support and assistance I received from her often went beyond her duties as a Social Worker. She helped me apply for a flat with a housing association and within a couple of weeks, I was given a two bedroom flat not far from Diane. Diane advised me to wait until the baby was born in order to move in. This meant that she could look after me for the first few weeks after the birth of my baby. Towards my due date, we were all getting excited. Peter and I spoke on the phone almost everyday. Gordon, my church minister, his wife Mary and their daughter Sophie kindly offered to do some baby shopping for me. I was amazed to see that their shopping for my unborn child included a posh, brand-new, two-in-one pram. "Wow!" is what I kept saying when they took me to choose the pram. By now, I had stopped going to college because the baby would be here anytime. However I promised to return in January.

MEETING THE FIRST BLACK PERSON

"Hello" a voice said behind me as I walked along the high street to do baby shopping.

"Hello" I said as I turned to see who was greeting me.

After more than a month of living in Fife, I was delighted and relieved to finally see a black face in the town. Fife didn't have many black residents when I had first arrived, and it sometimes worried me to see that I was the only black face in the whole town. This has since changed because there are more black people living in Fife now.

"Where are you from"? I asked curiously as I could see some of my tribe's features in her.

"I'm from Somalia. And you?"

"I'm from Rwanda."

After a great conversation, we exchanged contact details and have since kept in-touch. She encouraged me to become a member of Fife's International Women's Group which consisted of women of all nationalities. I soon became an active member and was later elected as the group's treasurer. My post as the group's treasurer meant networking and linking with many other Ethnic Minority Groups and voluntary organisations. The group somehow stopped meeting but a few of the women are my very good friends to this day.

IT'S A BOY!

It's the morning of 28th of October and I haven't had a good sleep. I have been having some pain on and off. By four o' clock in the morning, the pain gets worse so I shout for help and Diane comes running into my room. She immediately phones the hospital and speaks to the midwife who asks her to time the contractions.

"If the pain comes every five minutes then you need to get her here" the midwife said.

She runs a bath for me and I lay in it for quite a long time. It's about seven thirty and the contractions have become more intense and happen every three to five minutes so Diane rushes me to the hospital. She's by my side throughout labour.

Even though I have heard many stories about the pain of giving birth and have been to many antenatal classes, nothing could have prepared me for the pain of labour. I decline epidural and morphine because I want the birth to be natural. However the gas helps me very much. The labour goes on throughout most of the day. I don't want to eat or drink except cry, scream and swear at Peter who isn't even there to share my pain. At around three thirty in the afternoon, both midwives are convinced that the baby is ready to come so the hard work of pushing begins.

"Push!" they would all shout at me at each contraction.

"I can't do it, I'm too tired" I would scream back.

"Come on, you can do this!" Diane would say to try and cheer me up.

Even though I have been through the theory of how to push and midwives are still teaching me how to do it, I still fail to push properly. Now Diane takes it in her own hands to teach me so in very slow English, she explains what I should do but after so many attempts I still fail and by now the baby is getting distressed. Diane even gives me a little demonstration but end up bursting her waterproof sport's trousers. It's very funny to see her walk with her legs tightly closed due to the damaged trousers.

Just when the midwives are deciding to involve the doctor in order to conduct forceps, at six twenty in the evening, the baby's head pops out after an unspeakable effort in order to avoid the forceps. The following operation is much easier because at the next contraction the baby has arrived in his new world.

"It's a little boy" the midwife says as she put him on my chest.

I can't help but scream with shouts of joy. He's the most beautiful baby I have ever seen.

"Thank God" I said relieved to see that the battle is over.

I hold the baby for a very long time not wanting to pass him over for weighing and cleaning. Diane is in floods of tears too. It's such a special moment of my life even though I'm missing my whole family to share it with me. Diane immediately goes to the public phone in order to phone Peter. He too can't believe that he is a father now. I'm then taken to the ward and stay in hospital for a few days. That night Peter phones the hospital and all he can say is "I can't believe I'm a father."

We decide to name the baby there and then. I want Emmanuel because it means God with us but Peter wants Nathanael meaning God's precious gift. After some discussion we agree to call our precious son Nathanael.

On the fourth day, I leave the hospital and head to Diane's house where I am expecting to stay for a few weeks. I enjoy and receive a lot of support and help from her. The midwife comes to visit every day and her visits are expected to last ten days and then the health visitor will take over. The health care and support that I receive from NHS Fife goes beyond my imagination. Back home, those who can afford to have babies in hospitals only get the medical care in the hospital. Once you are out of the hospital, that's it. Perhaps mega rich families afford to pay for private nurses but these are a tiny minority. I feel very valued as a human being and am very grateful to the NHS staff for the care and support that I receive during this crucial period of motherhood.

MOVING TO MY OWN FLAT

In November 1999, I moved into my two bed room flat. The flat was new and modern. It was beautiful and I loved its kitchen and bathroom. Diane and a few friends helped with the decoration of a few rooms. I had bought some furniture and kitchen utensils. I continued to acquire furniture slowly but steadily and within a month I had almost everything that I needed. Friends also donated items which were very helpful. I found Fifers very kind, friendly and generous. I will never forget a friend whose elderly mother had died and left her a house full of things. She took me to her mother's house and said "please choose all that you want before I give anything to the charity shop". I was astonished because the furniture and ornamental objects were very good quality. I felt like taking everything. I replaced most of my old furniture by the good quality furniture that she had given me. If I were to put a price on gifts that I have received by friends and people in Fife, it would be in thousands of pounds. That how generous people are where I live.

Moving into my own flat was very hard work. Although I loved the idea of being in Britain, the challenges were great. I found the culture and life style very different. Often I felt isolated from the society because of the language and cultural barriers. It took me months to get to know my neighbours whereas back home you move into a street today and tomorrow everyone is there to welcome you. The only social life I had was going to the church, talking to friends and watching the TV. Shopping was different too. At home we shop at the market. There aren't supermarkets except in big cities. Even in cities, supermarkets are visited by rich people so I was surprised to see that here you did all your shopping at a supermarket. Very many things were new for me and it was like being a new primary school pupil who has to learn the alphabet and counting. Even things like disposable nappies and shampoos I had never seen before. Things that seemed very basic to Scots were like new discoveries to me. It was like landing on a totally new planet. It was a lot of learning. However I enjoyed it because I love learning new things.

In December, Peter and my sister Annie came to visit. It was magnificent to see my beloved husband again and I was very pleased to see my sister. At last I had some family with me. Peter stayed for four weeks and went back home due to his work. He loved his work and didn't want to just leave. Plus it paid him very well so he couldn't risk leaving his job without the guarantee of getting another one here. Annie stayed with me in order to help me with the baby whilst at College.

HNC IN ADMINISTRATION AND INFORMATON MANAGEMENT

"Come in" the deputy rector said, as the minister and I knocked on her door. After some chat she asked,

"What can I do for you?"

"Chantal was at Glenrothes College but can't afford the college fees so I wondered if there is any possibility to enrol her at your community college?"

This was a high school which catered for community college up to the Higher National Certificate level.

After checking my documents including my admission at Glenrothes College at the HNC level, she made an appointment for me to meet the course tutor.

Unlike Glenrothes College, the interview at the community college was very informal and simple. Luckily my English was a lot better although not of an academic standard. But I convinced the tutor that I would accelerate my English learning and work hard to succeed. She must have seen how desperate I was to study because she took me on.

In February 2000, I started my two year part-time course. The first year was extremely hard. The academic and business language spoken at the college wasn't easy. The computer and information technology which I wasn't used to was very much part of the course. I attended college once a week which gave me the rest of the week to do extensive English learning. I learned to be fluent in English at the same time as learning the course. Subjects of my course included Accounting, Administration management, Human Resources, IT etc

We then had our first assessments and after much hard work, I handed them in. I was very sure that I would fail them due to my lack of fluency in English. Shortly before the summer holidays the results came and to my delight I had passed them all. I had never been so proud of myself. The passes motivated me to work much harder.

In September 2000 my sister Annie decided to go back home to Rwanda. Luckily my God-sent angel, Mary offered to take care of the baby whilst I was attending College. However I found it very hard to be a single mother and attend college at the same time so I persuaded Peter to join us. He agreed and in December 2000 he moved to be with us. He had to leave Scotland every six months in order to renew his visitor's visa. Unlike me, he was a citizen of Tanzania so he couldn't claim for asylum in this country because Tanzania was very peaceful. His trips cost us a fortune but luckily he had saved some money and therefore was able to afford it.

MISCARRIAGE

I couldn't help but cry when I discovered that I was pregnant without planning for it. We weren't ready for another child. Peter had just arrived and was trying to settle - the fact that we both didn't have jobs made the news even harder to take plus I was about to finish my HNC and move on to do HND and was feeling sick all the time etc.

"Every child is a blessing; come on be happy" Peter would say.

Even though he wasn't planning for us to have another child, it didn't affect him as much as it affected me.

I became quite ill, feeling very sick all the time. I lost a great deal of the little weight I had. My doctor was very concerned and made investigations. All tests confirmed that there was nothing wrong with me except lack of appetite which was causing the rapid fall in weight.

One morning I woke up with a lot of blood on me. I phoned the doctor who advised that I must immediately go to the hospital. A friend drove us to the hospital and they immediately scanned me.

"I'm sorry to tell you that you've miscarried" the technician said.

"Why?" I asked, very upset.

"One in five women miscarry in this country and there are no apparent reasons." She explained.

Even though I had initially resisted the pregnancy, I was very upset to miscarry because I had grown to love the unborn baby. I loved the idea of Nathan becoming a big brother to a little girl or boy. I had become even more excited at the fact that there was going to be only a two years age gap between Nathan and the baby. Although the pregnancy at that stage was just in form of liquid and blood, the pain and sadness of losing it felt like losing someone very close that I had known before.

I underwent a small surgery and stayed in the hospital for a day and night.

The following weeks saw me very miserable because not only did I feel very upset that our baby had died but felt guilty that the miscarriage was probably the result of my attitude towards the early stage of my pregnancy. To this day I remember the baby on the date that I miscarried and on the date that it was due.

LEAVE TO REMAIN

It was March 2001 and almost sixteen months since I had last been called for a proper interview at the Scottish Refugee Council after the birth of my son. However there was no sign from the Home Office of my screening interview which is the next stage in the procedure. With the passing of most of my subjects so far, I anticipated gaining my HNC that June. My hope was to look for a job and continue studying on a part-time basis. However, lack of immigration status meant that I wasn't allowed to work in this country neither was my husband because he was on a visitor's visa - he too was waiting on my immigration outcome in order to apply for the same leave to remain as my partner. I had been intouch with my lawyer on many occasions but like me there wasn't much she could do. After speaking to one of my friends about my concerns, she advised me to see my local MP[4]. She knew that the MP had a surgery that week and I could just go and speak to him. I went along to the surgery and waited for my turn. Then the MP's secretary called me and I entered the office. As soon as I walked in, I recognised the face because I had seen it many times on the Television. It was like meeting a Hollywood star. Since TV dominates most households in this country, I found myself very much involved with the Television. I always wondered what it would feel like to meet one of those people I saw on TV and there he was in front of me, the most powerful man in Scotland. It felt great to meet the then Scottish First Minister. I was almost shaking and didn't know how to greet him or what to say. It took me a few minutes to pull myself together in order to tell him why I was there. I had Nathan with me and the First Minister spoke to him. T He promised to write to the Home Office in order to follow up the case.

Within a few weeks of his letter to the Home Office, I was called for the screening interview. At the interview they gave me a temporary work permit which meant I could now look for a job. Peter was there to take care of our baby so there was no reason for me not to get a job.

In June 2001, I was very blessed to secure the first job that I had applied for with a local pharmacy. I worked as a part time Sales Assistant. Even though I liked it, I didn't get the same job satisfaction I had when working in the office, so after successfully completing my HNC course, I embarked on the journey of searching for an office job.

"Hello" he said

"Hi, what's up?" I asked wondering why he'd phone me at work

"Well, there is a special delivery here for you and on the envelope it says Home Office. Shall I open it?"

At the sound of "special delivery" and "Home Office" my heart started to beat faster than normal, because I knew it was to do with my immigration outcome. I said "Yeah open it, you know you don't have to ask me before opening my mail."

Peter was teasing me because he knew very well that he was allowed to open all my mail. Anyway after teasing me he said,

"Oh, no!"

"What?" I gasped as my heart started to beat even faster

"It's a refusal."

"What?" I repeated again as if I hadn't heard him right."

"I said, it's a refusal."

"It can't be! how and why? Have they given any reasons?"

By now I was shaking with shock, because I had just settled in this country and so far was doing quite well, so I couldn't bear the thought of being sent back home - not yet anyway, because I needed my degree.

"Come on, I'm only joking" he casually said.

"Thank God for that. So what is it then?" I replied

"They have given you exceptional leave to remain until 2005"

"Praise God" I said relieved to hear that I had been given four years of leave to remain which was long enough for me to complete my degree.

THE OFFICE JOB

My search for an office job became the hardest thing I ever had to do since arriving. I must have posted more than a hundred applications without even being called for an interview. It was quite demoralising. Then I learned of a project which helped ethnic minority people in their quest for employment. I met the project manager who helped re-do my curriculum vitae. She also promised to send me any suitable job advert.

In September 2001, she posted me a job advert for a full time Admin. Assistant with the local interpreting service. I applied for the job hoping that my HNC in Administration and Information management combined with my involvement with Black and Ethnic Minority groups would give me at least the chance to be called for an interview. A week later I was over the moon to receive an invitation to attend the interview.

At the interview I gave it my best but was still not very confident with my English so I thought I didn't stand a chance. At the end of the interview, the panel promised to get in-touch as soon as possible. My interview was at two o' clock in the afternoon and at about four thirty in the afternoon; Peter received a phone call from the interpreting service as I had gone back to work. He immediately phoned me to give me the good news,

"The interpreting service's manager has just been on the phone" Peter said.

"What did she say?" I nervously asked,

"You've got the job."

"You must be joking!" I said.

"They will send you a confirmation letter very soon."

My God, this was another miracle to see that I had gotten an office job which I had badly longed for. I handed my notice to my employer and started my new job within a couple of weeks. Today I'm still working with the organisation and I love my job very much. I love the fact that the service's aim is to help non-English speaking people to have equal access to services without the language barrier. Having been there myself, I know how difficult it can be to live in a country where you don't fluently speak its language. Besides my administrative tasks, I also interpret in Kinyarwanda, French, Swahili and Lingala.

In 2002, I decided to apply for a part time HND course in Administration and Information Management at Fife College. I was given two options: to either study part-time HND course for two years or take the much harder but shorter route of Diploma in Administration Management course by distance learning with the Institute of Administration Management (IAM) London. Although the latter was harder in terms of course modules, it would take only a year to gain the diploma which is equivalent to HND. The course would be supervised and delivered by Fife College Lecturers in collaboration with IAM London. Students had to choose a specific project and produce a report which included recommendations at the end of the course. After much thought and consideration, I enrolled on the IAM diploma course because I wanted to get my diploma in a year rather than after two years. Luckily my employer was undergoing changes moving from a manual to computerised system - it was a golden opportunity to work on such a project. The organisation's management kindly allowed me to produce a report based on the benefits of having a computer system in the service. It was another great challenge. I was used to assessments which were quite straightforward. Writing a proper report arguing my case wasn't going to be an easy job. I worked with both lecturers and my employer to put my work together. A class mate called Una who is now one of my best friends also provided me with enormous help assisting with my research work. Another friend assisted me by going through my work to ensure that the grammar was right. I went to college every Tuesday evening studying from six till nine in the evening.

In June 2003, I was delighted to pass my project. I was later that year awarded the International Diploma in Administration Management.

AT LAST – A DEGREE!

Shortly before the end of my Diploma course, tutors presented us with the next steps. Students who would successfully complete their diploma had the opportunity to apply for the third year of BA Administration Management course with the University of Abertay. Students had the option to do the course on a part-time or full time basis. This was a life time dream so I applied for the course. My course tutor and employer provided excellent references and I was delighted to be admitted to the part-time course starting from September 2003. The course would take two years to complete and I had to attend College every Tuesday and Thursday from six till nine in the evening. Working full-time combined with having a young child meant this was going to be very hard indeed but it was an opportunity that I had been waiting for all my life.

In September I started the course and found that there were five of us in the class. The fact that I was looking forward to this all my life made it easier for me to concentrate because I needed to pass and give it my best. My office administration experience made it a lot easier for me to understand some of the lectures. However I found Employment & Company Law, Financial & Management Accounting and Database Design extremely hard. Luckily the lecturers were wonderful and helped me every step of the way. They were patient with me since I wasn't familiar with this country's law and financial systems. My class mates were the best. Whenever things got on top of me, I would call for help and they were all very, very helpful. Without their help, I would have found it too hard. It was the busiest two years of my life. When the results of our first assessment arrived, I wasn't sure that I would pass. You can imagine my joy when I found out that I had passed with merit. It was very encouraging and motivating.

A few months before the end of my course, I was delighted to discover that I was pregnant after trying for another child for almost two years. It wasn't easy to attend college with feelings of sickness and tiredness. But there was no way I was going to give up my course with only three months to go. So I had to be brave and keep on studying. Luckily the more exams and assessments we did the better results we all achieved. At the end of my course I needed one B to pass my degree with distinction. I wasn't convinced that I would achieve a B since I did my last exams under great difficulty. I had done three exams so my prayer and hope was that I would have a B - if not, I would still celebrate very much if I passed my course, because all I ever wanted was a degree. When the results arrived through the post I asked my husband to open the envelope because I was too nervous to do it. When he did, I could see his face shining which meant I had passed even though I didn't know the grades. *"At least it isn't a re-sit."* I thought.

"Is everything ok? I eagerly asked.

"Yes, you've passed all your exams."

"Great, can I have a look?"

As I set my eyes on the letter, I couldn't help but cry with joy and relief. Not only did I complete my course and finally had the degree that I had longed for but I got the B I needed for distinction. I soon discovered that everyone in my class had passed their degree with distinction. It was wonderful news. Within a few weeks we all got together to celebrate our great passes. The graduation was scheduled for November 2005, a month after my due date. I very much looked forward to the graduation day. My parents were very proud of me and they too celebrated my achievement even though I wasn't there to share the moment with them.

IT IS ANOTHER BOY

After the miscarriage and long trial for another child, it was wonderful to discover that I was pregnant again. The first twelve weeks were very hard with a few scares. It was time to attend the twenty weeks scan. I didn't want to know the sex of the child but Peter and Nathan insisted on knowing so I reluctantly accepted. On the way to the hospital Nathan kept saying that he wanted it to be a boy so that he could play football with his brother. I didn't mind the sex because to me every child is a precious blessing. As the technician scanned my tummy, we all got excited because she was about to tell us the sex.

"It's a boy" she said.

"Yeahhhhhh!" Nathan shouted with joy.

"Three boys at home! What am I going to do with you guys?" I jokingly said.

"Can I play football with him when he is born?" Nathan innocently asked the technician.

"Yes darling, but you will have to wait until he is a little bit older" she replied

Peter was equally pleased. It was as if he had expected it to be a boy because there are more boys in his family than girls. We had in the past joked how hard it was to conceive a girl if you were married to a member of his family.

At five, Nathan couldn't understand why this baby was taking so long to come. He'd once, before I became pregnant asked if he could have a baby brother or sister. I said to him "let us pray and ask God for that." As we closed our eyes he prayed,

"Father God, give me a baby brother or sister, in Jesus name we pray amen"

When he opened his eyes he asked,

"Where is the baby?"

It was an unexpected question so I quickly explained that it would take time to get the baby.

As the baby started to move in my tummy, Nathan got more excited. We involved him as much as possible. We went baby shopping together and he chose clothes and toys for the baby. He even chose the name for his baby brother. He wanted to call him Danny so we all settled for Daniel. The baby was due on 8th October 2005 so we were all looking forward to that day.

WHY NOW?

"Darling I don't feel well" Peter said as he dropped me at work.

"It's probably the cold. I suggest you go home, call your work to tell them you aren't well and then make an appointment with the doctor."

"Ok." he said as he kissed me goodbye.

Peter had just signed a permanent contract with his employer as a teacher after years of trying to get a permanent post. Unable to secure a job in Information Technology which was his field of work, he went on to train as a teacher as there was more chance for him to get a job in teaching than in IT. After a year at the University, he graduated with a Postgraduate Certificate in Education. He went on to do a probation year at a local school and the same school later employed him on a permanent basis. He'd been there for two years and everything seemed fine except the usual teaching stress.

We as a family were doing very well. After years of hard work, we had both finally secured good jobs with good salaries. We had bought a beautiful three bedroom terraced house in a good area of the town. Peter had passed his driving test and was driving a nice little car. Despite some ups and downs, our marriage couldn't have been better. Nathan who was now in Primary two was doing very well at school. With another baby on the way and my degree finally here, life couldn't have been better - well for me at least.

Peter called me at work to say that he'd managed to get an emergency appointment with the family doctor. At lunch time I called home.

"Has the doctor said what's wrong with you?"

"She thinks it's a throat infection and has given me some antibiotics."

"You need plenty of rest too and I hope she's given you a sick line"

"Yes, she's given me a week."

I posted the sick line to Peter's work and went back to my work, as usual phoning Peter in between to find out how he was doing. I would pop home every lunch time to be with him.

Prior to Peter becoming ill, he'd developed the habit of asking silly questions such as "Do you believe in consequences of our past deeds? or what happens if you don't obey God's call?" He would often use me as an example saying that the fact that I had lost my virginity before marriage or the fact that I had fallen pregnant prior to our marriage meant that there will always be some kind of consequences. I used to be furious and would categorically tell him that what I did in the past had nothing to do with what I was now doing. "God doesn't curse me because I had sex with you and fell pregnant before marriage. As far as my religion is concerned I asked God to forgive me when I realised that I had been disobedient and He forgave me. I don't see how God would punish you and me now because of the past which He has forgiven us."

This kind of conversation often led to heated arguments with exchange of harsh words. Peter seemed very jealous of the fact that I had prior to meeting him had boyfriends. Whether it was love or jealousy, I found it hard to understand why he appeared not to trust me based on the fact that I wasn't a virgin when he'd married me. I was often in trouble for accepting lifts from male colleagues. However I'm the kind of person who looks on the bright side of things so I used to think *"well he must love me very much to be this jealous."*

12TH SEPTEMBER 2005

It's about 11.50am and I phone my beloved husband to find out how he's doing. I'm shocked to hear that he's too weak to utter a word.

"I'm coming now" I said shaking with panic and fear.

I rush home and on the way I can't think of what could have gone wrong only hours after he seemed to be recovering well from his throat infection.

At home I find Peter lying almost unconscious on the sofa.

"Wake up, come on open your eyes, it's me Chantal" I said shaking with shock, panic and disbelief.

He opens his eyes as he tries to say something. In order to keep him awake and find out what's wrong with him, I slowly drag him to the dinning room and sit him on the chair.

"What happened?"

"Tablets, I took a lot of tablets." he said sounding very weak.

I go to the kitchen where we keep tablets in one of the upper units only to discover that most tablets have gone.

"My God, what have you done, Peter? Were you trying to kill yourself?"

"No, each time I felt hungry I took tablets instead of food" he weakly said.

I ring for an ambulance which arrives in minutes and we rush Peter to the hospital. After taking his blood for tests, I wait in agony to know if any of his organs, mainly the liver, have been damaged by the overdose. Meantime he's given an injection to counteract the effects of the medicine. After hours of waiting, we are both relieved to hear that everything is fine. However the cause which has led him to taking the overdose is still unknown since he doesn't want to say much except it was an accident.

I spend hours with him because he's too scared to be left on his own. At around 10.00pm he reluctantly allows me to leave. Our childminder has been very kind to let Nathan stay with her overnight. As soon as I walk into my house, I fall down screaming like a baby. *"How could this be happening now? I'm about to have a baby and my husband decides to go now and leave me on my own with two children. How could he do this to me? What about Nathan and our unborn child? Did he not think of them when he was taking the overdose? What if he had died? What would I have told Nathan and the baby? Oh God why now? Why me? I don't have any family here? I'm heavily pregnant and physically tired. God how could you allow this to happen to us?"* That night I cried very much and was in such deep emotional pain that I thought I was going to go into labour but luckily it never happened.

Peter was discharged after a couple of days with no explanation of what was wrong with him as all tests had shown that everything was fine. This made it harder for both of us to understand. After another week of struggle on sick leave, we both agreed that it was best for him to return to work as it would bring some routine back into his life. By now Peter seemed to be very withdrawn and tearful. I still didn't understand what was wrong with him. It was the first time I'd ever seen Peter so distressed and tearful for no apparent reason. With only weeks to go before the baby was due, I couldn't help but wonder what would happen to us since Peter wasn't showing any sign of getting better. What made things worse was the fact that his illness was not physical but mental. We wondered if it was depression but we didn't believe in depression so we ruled it out. Peter went back to work and on the third day of his return to work, I received a phone call from him

"Where are you? I asked, worried that something was wrong, as I could hear he was not well.

"I'm at your car park."

"But I thought you were at work."

"Please come now because I'm not feeling well."

I rushed to the car park and found a tearful Peter with a bump on his forehead.

"What happened?" I asked.

"I was frustrated with myself so I started banging my head on the desk."

"What? In front of your pupils?"

"No, they had left. Then the headteacher passed and saw me. He noticed that I wasn't well and asked me to go home." he tearfully said.

"Oh darling come here." I said as I gave him a hug, relieved to hear that at least he hadn't done the banging in front of the children.

At home, I phoned the doctor for an emergency appointment and was lucky to have one. You must come with me Peter said as I suggested letting him go to the doctor's room on his own in case he wanted to discuss very personal stuff with her.

The doctor unfortunately couldn't understand what was wrong with Peter but wondered if it was a severe depression or some kind of psychological illness. She referred him to the psychiatrist and rang the psychiatric hospital for an emergency consultation. Peter was very reluctant to attend the hospital but the GP and I managed to persuade him to do so.

At the hospital the psychiatrist diagnosed him with severe depression and referred him back to the family doctor for prescription. The doctor prescribed him anti-depressants hoping that they would help him.

At home, we spent hours on the internet trying to see if we could dig more information on the illness. The symptoms described on the internet were similar to those experienced by Peter so there was no other explanation except for depression.

I started my maternity leave on 24th September 2005 and by then I was used to Peter's illness. Even though he'd been prescribed anti-depressants, he was getting worse rather than better. He became withdrawn and developed a phobia of the public and space. The usually smart Peter had become almost like a guy living in the jungle. He didn't shave and his usually neat short afro hair had grown and was kept untidy. It frightened me day and night to see my beloved husband go down hill without any proper explanation. I often wondered if I was the cause of his illness. Our personalities differed very much and I often felt that I wasn't the type of wife Peter had hoped to marry. Unlike many African women, I'm more outgoing, open minded and independent. Peter sometimes found it hard to deal with me because he's quit and calm. Throughout his illness, I kept asking him if I was the reason he was ill and he assured me that I wasn't. I was convinced that no one can become severely depressed without any reason but Peter wouldn't give me any. *"Maybe it's the stress of teaching"* I would often think.

After weeks of staying indoors, I managed to persuade him to at least go out at night for a breath of fresh air. So a few days before the birth of our baby, Peter started going to different parks at night. It almost became like a normal routine for him to go out at night. He used to stay there for hours and some of the times if he stayed for too long, I would get very worried that he'd been in an accident or killed himself. One night he came back and told me that God had spoken to him just as He had spoken to Moses.

"God is calling me to serve him."

"Good" I said.

"But we have many financial commitments; I can't leave my job just like that."

"God will provide because He is Jehovah Jireh." I said with confidence.

"It's not that easy; I have to seriously think about it" he replied.

"Whatever you decide to do, I shall support you a hundred percent."

I was ready to give up my comfort in exchange for Peter serving the Lord on a full time basis. I too had often heard the spiritual call to serve God but wasn't brave enough to leave my job. I encouraged him and said that I would keep my work while he was serving God. We decided to take our time and pray for the situation.

3ʀᴅ OCTOBER 2005

The whole house except the baby's room looked very untidy and the baby could be here any minute. I decided to tidy up the house starting with my bedroom. It had been ages since I had last tidied the house that way. By seven o' clock in the evening, I was exhausted but it was worth it because the house looked spotless. Peter couldn't understand where I had gotten the energy from. That night I went to bed early and when I woke up for my usual emptying of my bladder, I could feel some slight pain.

"Peter I'm feeling some pain similar to that of period pain."

"Do you think you are going into labour?"

"Maybe, let us wait and see." I replied.

I then went back to sleep but kept feeling very uncomfortable throughout my sleep because of the pain. At eleven o' clock, I was up with pain but it wasn't bad enough for me to call the hospital.

At two o' clock in the morning, I started bleeding and the pain was unbearable occurring every three to five minutes.

"Please phone the hospital" I said as I rushed to have a shower before heading to the hospital.

The hospital requested me to immediately go in as by now my contractions were coming every two to four minutes. Somehow we managed to get our friends to look after Nathan so that Peter could be with me.

At the hospital, I was screaming and crying in all the five languages that I speak. The midwives must have thought I was from another planet since not many people mixed their language like I was doing. I looked at Peter and could not believe his face; it was as if my pain didn't mean much to him. However he'd been emotionless for weeks so I didn't expect much sympathy from him.

At five twenty five in the morning, on 4th of October the baby safely arrived after a hard, painful but short labour. I was relieved to see that the baby was here much quicker than when I had Nathan. He looked angelic with big eyes and dark hair. He was very cute. Peter's face somehow lit up when he held the baby. He looked full of hope. I thought *"well this could be a breakthrough healing for him."*

I stayed in the hospital for a night and was home the next day. I received stitches and could hardly walk so Peter had no choice but to help. He helped with everything and for the next two weeks I was treated like a queen. But after a couple of weeks, Peter became distressed again, crying all the time and not wanting to do anything. I was back to doing everything. It felt like looking after three children but I had to get on with it.

The midwife came to see me for ten days and handed the visits over to the health visitor. On her first visit, the health visitor noticed that the midwife had ticked me as high risk for postnatal depression. I totally denied this and we both wondered why she had put me at high risk. Looking back I guess she perhaps saw how things were at home. Even though I was physically and mentally exhausted, I never counted myself as one of those who could easily be defeated by circumstances. After all, I had been through a lot and nothing could be worse than the uncertainty of life I had experienced throughout my childhood. However what made me mentally tired was the fact that I didn't share much about my burden with other people because I thought this was part of marriage and therefore had to be kept very private. I often told friends and family that Peter had suffered a terrible flu which had led to post viral illness - how long could I have kept on the secret of his depression was totally another issue. One thing that kept me going during this dark period was my two beautiful children. Seeing them both happy was like seeing a light in the middle of a dark tunnel. Nathan was very happy to see his little brother and kept sitting besides him all the time. Often he would want to skip school so that he could be beside his baby brother. It was wonderful to see them get on very well.

ULTIMATE BETRAYAL
17TH DECEMBER 2005

"Please bring me some Chinese food on your way back" I said as Peter left for his night walk.

"Ok" he replied.

With both children in bed, I lay on the sofa and watched the TV until eleven o' clock at night when Peter came back.

"Chantal I have something to tell you" he said, as he put the Chinese take away down and went on his knees.

"God has ordered me to confess something bad that I have done and I really don't know if you can take it" he said with tears running down his cheeks.

"Look, I have been through a lot recently so I don't see anything worse that I can't take in, so just get to the point please."

"I have been seeing other women."

"What do you mean?"

I often wondered how I would react if I found out Peter was having an affair. And there I was - not believing my ears as these words of confession came out of his mouth.

"Amongst the women I have been seeing are Rose and Sabrina."

"What? I exclaimed in disbelief as both girls were my friends.

Rose was the girl next door where I had first met Peter, and Sabrina was a good friend too. She had recently been studying for Masters at one of the Scottish Universities and I was very pleased to welcome her for weekend stays and visits to my house.

"No, this can't be true" I exclaimed.

"Yes I'm sorry to say that it is true."

"Also I passionately kissed Roberta."

"But she's the daughter of our best friend. How could you do this?"

This was like hearing a serial adulterer even though he later assured me that he hadn't had a full sexual relationship with any of these girls, and by that I didn't even know what he meant, because by now I was very sick that I didn't want to hear any details.

"Whatever relationship you had with them, it was unfaithfulness and betrayal." I screamed.

"Please forgive me; please forgive me because there are more stories."

"Elijah could be my son because both my brother and I slept with the same woman within a week" he continued.

I have never been calmer in my life. The more shocked I was at the stories I was hearing, the calmer I became which was frightening because it was as if I was losing touch with reality.

"Have you thought of a DNA test because if he's your son then you better start acting like a father and not abandon all the responsibilities to your brother" I calmly said.

After he'd finished talking I said,

"How could you do this to me? You have lied to me from the beginning and I feel like our marriage has been based on lies. I may have secrets that I have kept from you but they are no way as bad as what I have just heard."

By now I began to lose my temper,

"From the beginning you told me that you'd never touched a woman never mind sleep with them and have a child. How dare you lie to me after the way you treated me when you found out about my first boyfriend. I was so humiliated by you that I chose not tell you the rest of my love stories. Actually I had another few boyfriends after I separated from my first one. I couldn't have told you these things because I felt you would have probably buried me alive with jealousy. You have lied, lied and lied. You pretended to be a virgin and treated me like dirt and a prostitute. Even after we got married, you continued to torment me about the fact that I wasn't a virgin when you married me pretending that you were the clean and faithful one. You condemned me again and again about the loss of my virginity and you often judged my faithfulness to you based on that fact. After all that you have put me through, how dare you tell me that you have been with women all along. This is too much for me and I need time to think of my next move because you have told me too much today."

I have never felt betrayed, humiliated and hopeless in my life. "How could you?" is the phrase that kept coming from my mouth. I was in total shock and the trauma of hearing my husband's confession felt real. I hated him so much that the sight of him made me physically sick. I needed time to think about what I just heard. I felt that this was not the right time to take any decision although my immediate reaction and feeling was to get him out of my life there and then. But it wasn't an easy decision to take. With two children and a depressed man to care for I couldn't run away and hide in a retreat place because that what I felt I wanted to do. My only retreat place was one of the rooms in our house so I asked him to leave me alone. I locked myself in the study and couldn't come out for a few days.

From that moment I sank into a different world; a world of mind. I searched deep within me to see if I had the courage to forgive Peter. The deeper I went inside myself, the farther away I went from reality. Suddenly thoughts started to run inside me like a fast train. I have never experienced anything like this before. I stayed in the study room for almost three days not eating. Because I was breastfeeding I had to drink milk so I drank lots of it. I had my bible and gospel music with me. I prayed and cried to God to show me the right way since I felt completely lost. Then I phoned mama saying that I was dead. I saw myself flying without wings and I could see my own dead body from above. It was an experience that I will never understand but apparently it's all part of the illness that I was later diagnosed with. She panicked and spoke to Peter who explained to her that I was not feeling well.

CHRIST MASS NOT CHRISTMAS

We had been invited to spend Christmas with my minister and his family. We were all looking forward to spending Christmas together for the first time. Although the minister and his family had become more than a family to us, we always spent Christmas day with Diane and her family because she had told us from the beginning that Christmas is her favourite day of the year and that she loved spending it with family and special friends like us. But this year we felt it was right to be with our minister and his family.

By Christmas Eve, my mental state was quite unstable. I was moving back and forward between reality and visions. The visions were so clear at the time that to me they were very real. I kept travelling in the past, present and future. Whenever my mind went deep in past, I saw clear visions of the Stone Age, slave trade, colonialism, old testament etc. Sometimes I was back in the present and sounded and acted very normal as if there was nothing wrong with me. Sometimes my mind travelled in the future. In the future I saw visions of life after death. I was flying without wings and I could see my own body from heaven. It was a very weird but pleasant experience. Because of my strong faith in God, I was convinced that I now resided in heaven on earth (paradise). I saw clear visions of Jesus sitting on the throne and I heard from Him many times. I was shown a very healthy heavenly bank account where I was told to just withdraw any amount whenever I wanted. I thought that I had met people like Billy Graham, Richard Branson, and Bill Gates etc. In my visions I even met people who had died before and were now residing in heaven. The people that I met included members of my family such my grandparents and uncles, Derek Prince who had a Christian Ministry etc.

I started to write in shape and numbers. I believed God had given me a contract to write and publish "Shalom Code" in response to the "Da Vinci Code" which had just been published. I heard a clear voice which I believed to be from God saying that the Da Vinci code was a total blasphemy. I strongly believed that God was not happy about the Da Vinci code book and therefore wanted to use me in order to publish a book of truth. Some of what I believed at the time to be the manuscript of "Shalom Code" included writings such as Christ mass not Christmas, worship not war ship, L for love not Lust, P for power and peace not passion for sex etc.

After a few days in this state of mind, I decided to talk to Peter. I explained to him that I had very much forgiven him and I stated my reasons for doing so. I was very happy to have been able to forgive Peter and felt at peace. However my mind was still running back and forward in time. He took it upon his own hands to look after us because it was evident that I wasn't thinking rationally most of the time. He was quite reluctant to allow me to seek medical help since we both thought it was just the shock of what I had heard which made me ill.

On Christmas day I felt that I was well enough to be with our friends. When we arrived everything seemed fine until dinner time. The table was full of food including a delicious looking turkey. Nathan who by now was filled with scripture verses was preaching instead of eating. Soon after eating the starters, Nathan asked to be excused and went into the sitting room. I supposed he had seen and heard so much. He too was finding it hard to live with two mentally unstable parents. At one point he was the one reminding us to feed them as we were always lost in our unreal worlds; Peter in his low one and I in my high one.

I too asked to be excused as I followed Nathan into the room into the sitting room. Mary followed us and that's when I did burst into tears. Tears were followed by speeches coming from my irrational thoughts. The Christmas which we were all looking forward to spending together, turned into a living nightmare for our hosts, who didn't have a clue about my illness prior to our visit. After hours of what can only be described as psychiatric dealings by our hosts we managed to leave.

At home I couldn't sleep as thoughts became more irrational. I heard voices and saw images of slaves and was convinced that this practice was still going on today. I told Peter to pack our bags and leave as I could no longer cope with living in the country of colonisers and slave buyers. What had happened many years ago suddenly seemed to be happening in the present. He too was mentally unstable and agreed with me so we packed that night. As I realised the extent of my mental instability, I phoned for an ambulance and was taken into the hospital. The medical doctor referred me to a psychiatric doctor who diagnosed me with baby blues meaning postnatal depression. He discharged me and asked me to see my family doctor for a prescription. I never did until things got out of hand.

At home, I continued to live between two worlds - the real and unreal one. Hearing voices and seeing visions became very frequent. Everyday, my divine appointment by God to serve and work for him became clearer. However as a sinner, I felt very unworthy to serve a Holy God. I entered into serious discussions with God asking him to leave me alone since I wasn't worthy of serving him. Then a clear voice suggested something in order to solve the problem - I was to baptise myself and my family, die and rise again as a new creature with the power and confidence to serve God. That day, I filled the bath and baptised first the baby and Nathan and then myself. After the baptism, I was told by the same voice to leave the house naked - meaning that I was leaving my old me inside the house and showing my new me outside. Earlier that day, Peter had been thrown out and was sitting in his car in order to observe the situation. I took both Nathan and Daniel to Peter in the car and went back inside the house. Next, I emerged from the house naked, walking towards our street. It was a freezing day in January and it had snowed heavily - yet I felt warm, supernatural and powerful. Peter who was in the car with the children who were only half dressed, watched in horror as he saw me walking naked. Within a few minutes of this drama, my friend Claire arrived by coincidence. She ran towards me and took me to her car, not understanding what was going on since she hadn't been aware of my condition. After clothing me with her jacket, she rang for an ambulance - luckily the children and I were found to be well. That day, Claire kindly took me and the children to stay with her so that she could keep an eye on me. The following day, Peter collected us and we tried to put the weird experiences behind us. However this was just the beginning of a terrible illness - psychosis.

Shortly before our illnesses, we had been given a loan for home improvements. The next few weeks saw me spending these thousands of pounds like mad. First I bought a few bottles of red wine and poured it all over the house thinking that it was the blood of Jesus to clean my house as Peter had admitted to having kissed my friend in the house. Then as the house became very messy, we had to leave and stay in a hotel. We stayed in the bridal suite of a very expensive hotel but who cared, as I seemed to think that I was richer than Catherine Zeta Jones or Victoria Beckham. My heavenly wealth was limitless - well so I thought at the time. Even though it was all like a dream, I lived it because we had about ten thousands pounds in our account and to me it was just a 0.000001% of my heavenly bank share. I was convinced that when my Bank of Scotland account ran out; God would just put more cash in it. I later learned from my doctor that this is known as a retail therapy condition. I shopped like a super star buying designer clothes for me and my children, lots of expensive perfumes, bags, clothes etc. I went and bought myself the latest laptop and desktop. We even bought a brand new seven seater car - on loan ofcourse. The whole experience was surreal. I was under the impression that I was now destined to lead a very grandiose life because I was very sure that I had now been employed by God as one of His chief executives and writers. I was writing things about the Middle East and African conflicts, the truth of the bible, the corruption of the world's leaders etc.

Today I look back and see that most of the things I wrote at the time of my illness don't make sense but some of them do.

We stayed at the hotel for weeks and one day, I told Peter that I wanted to take Nathan on a day trip. He reluctantly allowed me and asked me to keep in-touch by mobile telling him where I would be since I didn't know exactly where I was going.

13TH JANUARY 2006

At the bus station, we boarded the bus to Glasgow. I'd about nine hundreds pounds with me so I could afford my royal life. In Glasgow we went to one of the city's five star hotels and booked in for a night.

Afraid that Peter would report me missing and the police could contact all hotels in Scotland to trace me and Nathan, I booked using one of my many middle names. My name here was Chantal Mukozi. I paid some cash in advance and was shown my room. The room was very posh and perfect. Nathan and I ordered our lunch. I also booked myself for a hair and beauty treatment. I did some clothes shopping and so could afford changing every hour. In the corridor, Nathan and I played martial arts pretending that we were power rangers. I must have done it so well because the waiter who brought our lunch was quite impressed. He was a mixed race handsome young man. I started chatting with him. As the conversation went on, I found myself saying,

"I come from a royal family in Africa and it's normal for us to train in martial arts for our defence."

"Yeah I can see that you're very good at it ma'am" he said, almost shaking with disbelief that he'd met an African princess.

"What's your name and where do you come from?" I asked

"My name is Ryan. My mother is Scottish and my father is from Zimbabwe"

"It's very sad what's happening in Zimbabwe. Listen I like you and I trust you because you're like my brother. What time are you going to finish work today? "

"I will finish at three o' clock, ma'am."

"Perfect! Could you please baby sit for me while I go for my hair and beauty treatment? I will pay whatever you charge me."

"Yeah that's fine, ma'am."

"Ma'am, what's your name?

"My name is Chantal. Please stop calling me ma'am, just call me Chantal right?"

"See you soon" I said as I watched in amazement the look on the waiter's face. It's as if he'd seen a millionaire.

At three o' clock, my new childminder was there. After handing him one hundred pounds for a couple of hour childminding, the guy couldn't have been happier. He kept thanking me all the time. Nathan wanted a play station2, so I handed two hundreds and fifty pounds to my new childminder and asked him to take Nathan to the city centre and buy him whatever he wanted.

I went to the salon and chopped my long hair and asked them if they could make me look like Paris Hilton. Everyone in the salon was laughing but I wasn't because I was serious. After the hair and beauty treatments, I looked like a million dollars.

I then headed to the BBC Scotland television office requesting them to give me interview on live TV. At the reception the guy put me on the phone to the editorial room.

"Can we help you?" the lady on the phone asked.

"Yes, I'm an African princess who is on holiday here" I said.

"What can I do for you?"

"I want you to interview me on live TV"

"Interview you about what?" she asked sounding quite puzzled.

"I want to speak about Africa and Asylum issues."

"Sorry madam, we are not currently doing anything like that."

"Ok" I said, as I put the phone down disappointed that I didn't get to go on TV as I had hoped.

I then headed to the "Evening Times" office with a piece of paper titled "press release". In it were a few words explaining about the Shalom Code, my imaginary book. I folded it and placed it in a journalism book that I had bought in Caledonia University Library upon our arrival in Glasgow that morning. At the reception, I handed the book to the lady sitting at the desk. I whispered in her ear that she'd seen a black angel who wanted to bless her with the book.

"I love this book because it helped me during my journalism course" she replied, looking quite amazed by what I'd just said to her.

"What's your name and where do you come from?"

I'd disappeared before she could finish the question. She came running after me but I was already in the black cab which was waiting for me outside. As I looked back from the cab window, I could see her browsing the whole complex trying to see if she could see me.

At the hotel, I found Nathan and Ryan waiting for me. After thanking my childminder, he left. Before going to the swimming pool which Nathan was very much looking forward to, we ordered some mid afternoon drinks and snacks. On the phone, the receptionist taking our orders said "okay Ms Makosi, the orders will be with you very soon". It was after I put the phone down that I realised he'd just called me Ms Makosi. I guessed Ryan, who had prior to leaving us told me that he had felt like he had just met a celebrity, probably told people that I was Makosi in disguise. Makosi is a black woman from Zimbabwe who had become famous after winning the third place in Big Brother six.

I didn't dispute the mistake because I wanted to see what would happen. The waitress who brought our snacks kept calling me Ms Makosi and I was happy to accept this new name. At the swimming pool people kept starring at me. After an hour or so, Nathan and I left for our dinner. I left my clothes in the cabinet and handed the key to the receptionist informing him that I had left my belongings in the cabinet as we planned coming back. With my dressing gown around me, we went back to our room for dinner. By now some people were following me wherever I went. It was as if they had seen a real celebrity. The place which seemed very calm and quite like heaven when we'd first arrived suddenly turned busy like a market. The corridor leading to my room was full of people staring at each move I made.

Back to the swimming pool, I found my clothes and belongings gone. I supposed Makosi's fans took them. I complained to the receptionist who asked me to complete a form about the disappearance of my belongings. I didn't want any hassle and waste of time so I never bothered to do anything about it.

At eight in the evening and after speaking to my mother and father, I lay down in my bed feeling quite relaxed after a hectic day. Nathan was playing his playstation2 when the phone rang. It was the receptionist; she wanted to know how I was going to pay for the bill which by now had run into hundreds of pounds.

"How dare you question my way of payment now after we'd agreed that I will pay you tomorrow when I check out" I said furiously.

"But madam, you've been using a lot of services and we just want some kind of guarantee like a bank card to ensure that payment will be made."

"Are you saying that I'm some kind of fraudster who won't pay her bill? Don't you know that my father owns this place? I am the heiress of this world's wealth. If it wasn't for my father, you wouldn't be in this job so who are you to question me about payment.

"Excuse me, I don't understand what you are saying," she replied.

"Of course, you don't understand what I am saying, because you think Paris Hilton is the heiress of a five star hotel like this one whereas

I am the heiress of all the world five star hotels. The universe, the world and all that's in it belong to God and God is my father which makes me the eligible heiress."

"Pardon me?" she asked sounding quite puzzled.

"Look, since you don't understand me and you probably never will understand me, I would like to speak to your manager now," I said as I stormed downstairs with Nathan by my side to speak to the manager.

At the main reception, I was seen by the security manager instead of the hotel manager whom I very much wanted to see. The fact that I was seen by a security manager made matters worse. I was angry and shouting that they'd insulted me and hadn't respected me not only as a customer but as the child of God who owns the entire place. By now my thoughts started to run faster and at that time everyone looked like a racist and an idiot to me. After creating some scenes in front of people, the manager finally came. He and his security manager started to panic as they realised that my behaviour was quickly changing.

"Call the police" I said.

"No, we don't need to call the police in order to settle this matter," the manager said.

"Well, call the ambulance then because I'm not feeling well."

"You're fine, you just need to calm down and listen to us."

"Give me one reason why I should listen to you after the way you treated me."

After what seemed to be an everlasting conversation, it was clear that we were getting nowhere. In fact the more we spoke, the more irrational my thoughts became so I decided to immediately leave because I could no longer cope with the irritation and nuisance that these two managers were causing me. Without any shoes or jacket, I stormed out of the hotel with Nathan on my back. The two managers came running after us to ensure our safety especially of Nathan. They pleaded with me to return to the hotel in order to sort things out but I refused. I ran and ran crossing Glasgow's busiest streets. Even though prior to crossing these streets, I ensured that there were no coming cars from both directions, it was still dangerous because I wasn't myself. The managers then tried to hold me in order to bring me back to the hotel by force - that is when I took my blouse off, screaming that they were sexually harassing me. Afraid that this serious allegation could sound true, they took their hands off me and kept running after me instead. Meantime the police had been called but were finding it hard to locate us as I was going along street after street. Nathan was petrified but I kept reassuring him that we were fine and needed the police's help. Poor Nathan was relieved to see the police. Apparently I'd been trying to cross the M8 when the police arrived. They arrested me and put me in their van's cell. One of the police officers took good care of Nathan who was very scared and tired. Inside the cell, I kept banging and complaining that they were treating me like a gorilla from the jungle locked in a zoo cage. I felt like I was the victim so why were the police putting me in this hell of a cell? But I was powerless and helpless to do anything. They drove me to their station where they were advised to take me to the hospital for psychiatric assessment. Meantime the police, family and friends in Fife were all relieved to hear that both Nathan and I were found safe. Peter had reported us missing so it was good news to hear that we were found safe. At the hospital, I was admitted to the psychiatric ward. The police kindly took good care of Nathan until friends came from Fife to collect him and bring him back home.

PSYCHOSIS

I stayed in the psychiatric ward until the following day when I was transferred to Stratheden Hospital in Fife. During my stay in the psychiatric ward, I was convinced that the medical team was trying to eliminate me so that my imaginary book "Shalom Code" would never be published. They gave me medication to make me sleepy and it scared me to see that my overactive brain was becoming very sleepy and tired. I phoned my Rwandan friend in England pleading with her to get me out of the hospital because nurses and doctors were trying to kill me like they had killed our king Rudahigwa. King Rudahigwa was a much loved Rwandan king who according to Rwandan tales was killed by Belgians. The allegation has never been proved but the king's death remains mysterious to this day.

The following day, the ambulance took me to Fife. There were two nurses who came with me - I bet they had never seen anyone like me throughout their career. I was mad at them for treating me like a patient so to express my anger I spoke to them in sign, body language and eye contact. During our two and half hours journey, I couldn't settle. That afternoon the sun was shining and throughout my illness I knew I belonged to God and felt supernatural. I was convinced God had sent the sun in the middle of winter to protect and guard me as I was one of His special envoys. I wanted to scare the nurses so that they would leave me alone because I didn't want to go to another hospital. I would look at the sun through the ambulance window. My eyes would look inside the sun for a minute or two and then I would look straight into the nurses' eyes with the power of sun light still in my eyes. It made me feel powerful and indestructible.

At Stratheden hospital in Fife, I didn't want to speak to anyone. It took the medical team a long time to get any kind of information from me. I was angry and frustrated at the fact that I was being treated as a patient instead of being treated as God's special envoy. I couldn't understand how my life suddenly changed from staying in posh hotels and spending a lot of money to being locked in a psychiatric hospital room. The room was one of those guarded by staff twenty four hours a day. I'd been admitted on a Saturday afternoon so I needed to wait until Monday before I could be seen by the psychiatrist consultant who could prescribe me any kind of medication.

On Monday, I was taken to see the consultant. I was quite shocked to see the number of people sitting round the table to assess me. There must have been up to seven people. The consultant asked me questions to try and get information from me. I found myself preaching to him about the grandeur and might of God.

"The same God who created the universe has asked me to work for him. From Christmas day I've been taking orders from one person only and that person is God" I said.

After giving my doctors and nurses a sermon, the consultant looked at me and said:

"I think your mind is playing games with you."

I couldn't understand what he'd meant by saying this. He went on to explain that I was suffering from a condition known as psychosis. The website defines psychosis as an illness that prevents people from being able to distinguish between the real world and the imaginary world. Symptoms include hallucinations (seeing or hearing things that aren't really there, or delusions), irrational thoughts and fears.

The consultant then prescribed me anti-psychosis medication. However, on the third day of my medication, I took a bad reaction. That day, I'd been allowed out of the hospital for a day. Shortly after my anti-psychosis injection, Peter came to collect me. We went to St Andrews and had a lot of fun. Within a few hours, my jaws started to involuntarily move sideways. Peter had to urgently take me back to the hospital as my left side began feeling numb. At the hospital, I could hardly move my left side. I couldn't speak properly as my jaws constantly zigzagged. The doctors and nurses rushed me to bed and gave me lots of sweet liquid which I presumed was the medication to counteract the effects of the injection that I had been given earlier. I fell asleep and woke up to a body feeling like it weighed twenty stones. I was put off the injection and given a different type of medication. I thank God that I survived the severe reaction because I do realise it could have gone very wrong.

I was discharged after eleven days but was re-admitted in February when I became very ill again. Shortly before my second hospital admission, I'd been having serious rows with Peter. For the first time in our marriage, we agreed to separate temporarily in order to give each other a break. Peter and Daniel went to stay in a hotel not far from us. Nathan and I stayed at home. However Peter found the separation very hard and begged me to have him back. Because I wasn't ready to put up with him, I declined his request. As a result, he decided to stalk me, phoning in the middle of night and entering the house in the middle of the night without my permission. This behaviour went on for a few nights and one night after his call, I decided that I had enough. Nathan was asleep upstairs when I went downstairs to the kitchen and opened the medical cabinet. I took all the medicines that were inside the cabinet and put them on the worktop in front of me. It was as if I had reached a crossroads - one to life and one to death - in fact, my mind had never been clearer about my options before. There must have been more than a hundred tablets in front of me as we had Peter's and my anti-depressants, some painkillers and some anti-histamine medication etc.

As I looked at the tablets, I couldn't wait to leave this world as I seemed to have had enough of it. Just as I was thinking about taking them,

"Nathan! What about Nathan who is sleeping upstairs? Are you thinking of him?" a voice yelled inside me.

"What about him?" another voice said.

"Well, you can't do this to him. How do you think he would cope for the rest of his life if he discovers your body in the kitchen when he wakes up?" the first voice said.

The debate in my mind went on for a couple of minutes when I suddenly realised that what I was about to do, was the most horrible thing that I could ever do to my family and friends. I immediately rang for an ambulance which took me to hospital after Peter arrived to look after Nathan.

During my illness I wrote a lot. Although most of the time my thoughts were irrational, there were times when my thoughts became rational. I tried to write my thoughts during these two very different times of my illness. Most of the time I tried to write my thoughts as clear as possible but it wasn't easy because often I could hardly tell the difference between fantasy and reality. Below are some of the things that I wrote between being rational and irrational.

SUPERSTAR

I'm a superstar in my own world. Coming from extreme poverty to where I am is just unbelievable. Whenever I look around me and what I have, I become speechless. Who in their right mind would have thought that I would be where I am today. Looking back, it's as if situations and circumstances around me had condemned me to a lifetime of poverty and misery.

BLACK ANGEL

On 21st January 2006, God sent me a black angel from Sierra Leone. I suppose I needed to see with my very own eyes that black doesn't mean curse, poverty, stupidity, inferiority, and Aids. Black is just a name given to one of the different colours that we have on earth. I was very wrong to think that black people are inferior, poor, ill, hungry and stupid. Actually they are rich in unity, love, hospitality, endurance, patience, and joy. I used to think that Sub-Sahara Africans are destined to live and die poor because they are black. To me black meant dark, demon, death etc. How wrong I was, because black is just a colour.

THE POWER OF THE INDIVIDUAL

In life we tend to formulate our own opinion which often differs from others' and that's where the problem exists. The key to peace, development and prosperity is not in WMD, Live8, G8, writing off third world countries' debts etc. The key lies in our hands. Each individual around the world has the power to stop wars, to feed the hungry and educate the poor. Lack of knowledge is causing the endless vicious circle of hate, poverty and civil conflict. Very few of us in this world ever stop to think how we are going to make a difference or make someone's world better. Sometimes, it just takes a few seconds to make a difference. For example a simple hello and a smile can make a huge difference to a depressed person or a pound can make a huge difference to a child in Niger or Sri Lanka.

GOD IS GOOD

God is good all the time and all the time God is good. God granted us life, mercy, love, peace, joy, strength and power when Peter and I were both very ill with depression. He used people to lift us in prayer and support us. Thank you, Jesus, for creating us and making us part of one big family. Please guide us in our everyday walk with you. Show us how to reach those in great need and make us share your resources equally and fairly, especially with those in extreme poverty and wars.

I AM JUST A HUMAN

I'm just a human not a mountain
I'm just a human not an animal
I have feelings but mountains do not have feelings
I'm just a human not an ocean. Oceans have fishes and other creatures but I have a brain which holds an ocean of information.
"We need information from you so that we can help you" the nurse kindly said. That was the beginning of my healing.

ALTERNATIVES

God gives true freedom. God will use anything to make us happy, satisfied and peaceful. At the end of the day there are so many alternatives, for example when you go to a supermarket you have different brands to choose from for one product.

At around seven o' clock this morning, I asked for a cup of hot water and the staff said "I will give you water at eight thirty because that what the rule says"

I decided to use a plastic glass besides my bed and drew water from the hot tap in the washing basin and had my drink. It's about opening your eyes to alternatives!!!!!!!!!

GLOBALISATION

Why do wars, starvation, lack of education, lack of basic health provision etc still exist in an era when man is landing in space? The world spends trillions of dollars on military and space programs. Developed countries spend billions of dollars on health conditions caused by obesity and overweight yet on the other hand children are starving to death in developing countries. We are one world and must take responsibility for one another. We are living in an era of globalisation and must therefore globalise everything not just business. On the other hand, business globalisation could be the key to ending extreme poverty because mega companies are creating jobs in third world countries.

LIFE IS BEAUTIFUL

Life is beautiful and worth living,
   Love is wonderful and worth experiencing,
   Success is sweet and worth pursuing,
   Music is soothing and worth listening to,
   People are good and worth knowing.

I AM NOT USELESS

I'm on this world for a purpose,
   My destiny is to succeed,
   My star is big and very shiny,
   I can do it and yes I can do it,
   Of course I can do it,
   Actually life is fun and full of fun - that's if you choose to see it
that way,

Life is sweet - actually it's all about satisfying your inner being,

I love others very much and I think I'm not at all useless,

God has put me on earth for a purpose,

Only I, with the help of the Holy Spirit and others can fulfil what He has called me to do on earth. I choose to believe in God Almighty Creator, of the universe.

I choose to trust God and I choose to love and adore Him.

He is my true lover and my true companion. He's there for me even when I think He is not there. He is my guide and my salvation.

He is my everything, my true love and my true salvation. He is all I need and all I want. He is the giver of life.

Today I dance and sing because He led me out of Egypt.

I'm rescued and free - sweet freedom, sweet rescue.

In my slavery I cried to Him and He heard me. I belong to the creator of the universe.

FOR NATHAN MRIMI

He's just a child, my Hero

He's just a child, my Deliverer

He's just a child, my Saviour

He's just a child, my God

He's just a child, my Lord

He's just a child, my King

He's just a child, my Creator

He's just a child, my Love

He's just a child, my Provider

He's just a child, my Father

He's just a child, my Holy Spirit

He's just a child, my Peace, Strength and Joy

I saw God through Nathan

I spoke to God through Nathan

I felt God through Daniel

I received from God through both my precious beloved children Nathan and Daniel. He told me that I don't have to be in heaven in order to see Him. If it wasn't for Him, I don't know where I would be today. I would have probably been burning in hell. It exists, you know! I saw it with my very own eyes and thank God I wasn't in it. I was as far away as one can be. I was high up in heaven, beyond Mount Kilimanjaro, beyond the Himalayas, beyond the skies. I was chatting to the sun, moon and stars. My Lord showed me my house. It was a huge manse like the one on the framed picture that Mary gave us on Christmas day. My son Nathan was the sun that shone upon my life throughout my journey to heaven. He guided me, led me, and spoke for me and listened to me. Where I was unable to do something, he did it for me. I thank God for giving me, a simple and humble woman, such a bright son to the point where his brightness shone when my world was very dark. His quick thinking and advice kept me from the train of death and led me to the train of life instead. That's why I am here today. In this book, I call you Nathan Emmanuel Mrimi because you are: "GOD WITH US"

FOR DANIEL MRIMI

He's just a baby, the blessings' bearer
    He's just a baby, the author of this book
    He's just a baby, the light of my life
    He's just a baby, the bearer of good news
    He's just a baby, the holder of the key to wisdom
    He's just a baby, the cause of my joy
    He's just a baby, the head of my family
    His name is Daniel Samuel, the prophet of my household. He's very cute and calm. His calmness and innocence teach a lot. Unless you choose to ignore him, there's so much that this little cute baby can offer. Open your eyes and see!

WAR AND REBELLION

Give me one reason why killing an innocent person is very important to you. Is it because you want to be in charge? Is it because you fear for your life? Is it because of land? Is it revenge? Or is it because you want to better others? No matter what your reasons are, it doesn't justify the killing of innocent people. Every life is very precious and priceless. Nobody has the right to end another person's life. I expect human life to end naturally. If you really care for me so much that you want to fight in order to get me justice, why not do it peacefully? Why kill my father, mother, sister, brother, uncle, aunt? Think about Jesus and his disciples; think about Ghandi, Mandela, and Martin Luther King etc. They all fought peaceful wars and eventually won them.

Africa! The blood of your innocent people is flowing. Its flowing noise is becoming louder and louder. It's screaming for help, not for itself because it's too late now, but for its survivors. When will you listen to my pain? When will you put your arms and weapons down? When will you think of me? Do you think that I didn't have the right to live? What did I do to deserve death? I wanted to live; I wanted to grow old and see my grandchildren, I wanted to make a difference, I belonged to this world and had just as many rights as you do. But you decided to prematurely end my precious life. How could you sleep at night knowing what you did to me? My children are deprived of their parents because of you. Now is the time to at least honour my death by laying your arms and weapons down. You must overcome your selfishness and accept responsibilities. Remember that your days are numbered on this earth too, so why kill? If you really care, you must find peaceful ways to fight your cause. Don't use violence because enough blood has been shed. Think about the orphan! Think about the widow! Think about the widower! Think about a mother losing her child! Think about a father losing his child! Please stop now!

GREED AND CORRUPTION

You've been given the power to rule and lead. You've been chosen to be in charge. You've been called to serve your people. Your destiny is to guide, protect and help your people and that's why you are in charge. You are in charge not to amass great wealth and power! You are in charge not to build a family empire! You are in charge not to only advance your own family and friends! You are in charge not to be corrupt! You are in charge not to be served! You are in charge not to be treated like an emperor or king! You are in charge to serve your people in a fair and just way. You've been entrusted people's lives. You must remember that if a child dies due to lack of medicine while you are driving in cars which cost thousands of dollars then you are responsible for the child's death.

Oh Africa, please open your eyes
Please wake up and fight for your cause
For your helpless people have suffered long enough
Enough to last them a lifetime of recovery if you were to rescue them now
Your people need you
You can no longer afford to allow greedy and corrupted leaders rule over you
When will you take up your quit weapons and fight for the justice of your people?
When will you start the peaceful fight to rescue your people from extreme suffering?
Is it not time for you to act?
Is it not time for you to sacrifice all that you have for the sake of your people?
Wherever you are, please do something
The suffering of your people can't go on this way
I know you can do it, yes I do
You have the resources and brain
All you need is the will, passion and determination
Oh Africa, please open your eyes
And rescue your longsuffering people.

The topic below and some other topics above on Africa and corruption represent my thoughts when they were rational. These topics were things that had frustrated and bothered me for years and it just felt right to express my ideas in writing.

EDUCATION, EDUCATION, EDUCATION

How can a nation develop without investing in its young people's education? How can a society be developed and move on from extreme poverty and ignorance if it doesn't invest in its young people's education? How will the vicious circle of poverty be broken if young people don't set up reasonable goals of learning and attending schools. The accumulation of academic knowledge is priceless and is one of the only few solutions to today's equation of how to overcome extreme poverty in Africa. Without it, Africa will continue to go backwards, and people will continue to accept some of the most unacceptable behaviour of their leaders which include corruption, abuse of human rights and dictatorship. Africans must take their own cause in their own hands rather than waiting for international help all the time. The way to self sufficiency will be through personal development and advancement in each individual's mind and not always through international aid and the UN. Unless we Africans understand that it takes one's own effort in building and learning, society and the environment will not change. Major changes are required in ways of life too. Some of the culture is still keeping people back rather than encouraging them to learn and embrace the culture of academic curiosity and research. For example, there are many parts in Africa where girls aren't encouraged to study and learn, instead they are brought up and prepared to serve their husbands and children. It is as if women have no part to play whatsoever in an academic and technological world. These practices, seen as part of life in many parts of Africa must somehow change and people, in both urban and rural areas, must embrace the culture of learning and researching.

A well educated mind, not only builds society but fights the abuse of human rights and works towards the betterment of fellow humans. However, the education needed in young Africans is not only academic, but basic values of democracy and respect for human rights must be taught at a very young age. Young people are the future of any nation and unless one invests in their minds, there is no hope for total economic and social development. The sooner we start investing in young people's minds, the more chance we have for a better society and nation.

It's very hard to send your child to school when there's nothing to eat at home but believe me, it's possible to survive the hunger and send your child to school at the same time. Most Africans are blessed with fertile land which means parents could grow crops and educate their children. For example: despite being extremely poor, my parents decided to educate me at a very young age. When others were kept at home due to either lack of funds for school or society's norm of using children to work, I was lucky enough to be attending school. I'm very grateful to my parents because without this early emphasis on the importance of education, my life would have ended up in the vicious circle of extreme poverty. This means I would have probably been married at a very young age of fifteen or sixteen to a fellow uneducated poor guy, had children in this environment and the same would have happened to my children. Unfortunately this is the sad reality in Africa. Parents and adults need to start taking serious responsibilities when it comes to their children and young people's education. The government must play a huge role too. Campaign about educating children and the provision of affordable schools must be at the heart of any African government policies if they are to be developed. The government must understand that not only is education needed but it is an essential part of young people's lives because it broadens their mind and therefore prepares them for the future. A well educated society will work towards the building of a nation not the tearing of it. Education creates many opportunities too. These include a stronger economy because some people research, others become entrepreneurs, more jobs are created because educated people come up with initiatives and creative ideas etc. The spirit of research and independency must be encouraged rather than always accepting inventions from other parts of the world. People's minds are all the same when born; it's the way they are brought up that creates the difference in them when growing. Therefore it's not always where you are born or the colour of your skin nor the religion of your parents that determines what you're going to be tomorrow, but rather the way your mind is fed, the information around you and self determination for success. I remember in my life, there reached a time when we as a family didn't have a clue where our next meal would come from nor did we know where we were going to go next because of constant evictions, and yet my parents insisted on giving us what they knew was best for our future, in order to not experience the same kind of poverty they were experiencing. What they gave us was encouragement to attend school and do well. They always made sure that our homework and revision for our exams were done on time and neatly. I remember papa saying; "people, wars and poverty can take so much away from you, but one thing no one can take away from you is the knowledge that you accumulate during your learning process." Wow, what a powerful statement! This kind of speech from papa always encouraged us, because although society and government couldn't care less about our education, I started developing a self hope and determination to succeed, because I knew if I could study well and perhaps become a doctor, journalist or politician, my life would not have to be as poor as now. And so from an early age, I developed a strong interest in studying and learning in often unbearable conditions. Mostly, I used to do my home work using the moonlight because my parents couldn't afford to buy paraffin to burn the lamp. Often, we went to school with nothing in our stomach. However, the contemplation of a better future once I completed my education kept me going. And yet I know children who gave up school because there was no food at home or it was too long to walk or they simply felt it would do them no good because the government was corrupt anyway. Whatever reasons they had, it wasn't an excuse because today they are stuck in poverty and lack of knowledge, whereas students who carried on and did well are far better now. It's a fact that we (Africans) and our leaders must embrace with both hands that nothing will help us out of extreme poverty unless we decide to start taking education seriously.

The idea of educating all children to at least the level of Primary school and first four years of secondary school in developing countries is great. It sounds expensive and almost impossible to achieve and yet it's one of the easily achievable goals compared, for example, to accumulating massive amount of weapons and arms. It's my sincere prayer and hope that in the near future, every African child whether born in a remote village such as Shyira (Rwanda) or a mega city such as Johannesburg (South Africa) will have access to primary education and where possible to the first four years of secondary school. It's achievable and it has to start with ourselves.

The efforts to educate all children in Africa must be collective from parents and communities to governments. The time for only big, posh strategic talks from leaders must end and action to work towards the education of all children must start now. I do acknowledge and appreciate efforts made so far, thus the education of many Africans, but it's not enough and that's why we have conflicts, poverty, starvation, wars, diseases etc. The road to peace map and prosperity in Africa will be through education. This is so because it's very easy to corrupt and brainwash an uneducated, illiterate mind as it's narrow and ignorant, whereas it's very hard to do the same to a truly educated and literate mind as it is broad and informed. Today, more than ever, we must work with young people in order to build their tomorrow. Every child must be given a chance to live and learn. Cultural and social programmes must be put in place too in order to teach young people about respecting and tolerating others even if they do not come from the same background. Everyone in his/her corner must do something to work towards the idea of education. African governments must seriously start funding local projects that encourage learning and researching.

How do we fight injustice and corruption that has swept almost the whole continent of Africa? How do we move from the climate of conflicts, extreme poverty, epidemic diseases such as HIV Aids etc? How do we work towards better and developed nations in Africa? The answer to these questions is simply the education of young minds. A young mind well trained and well educated, will serve a society better and will be useful to the whole nation. Africans must embrace learning with all that they have, even if it means selling their possessions to educate their children. The key to tomorrow's development and economic growth lies with every family who have young children. The time has come for African governments and communities to concentrate on the provision of better schools, libraries, learning and research centres and good universities. The strategy of feeding young Africans' minds with knowledge is so vital if the continent is to succeed in making poverty history. Locally, nationally and internationally, everyone must work towards this huge goal of educating every single young person in Africa. If you look at India, China and Japan today, their development isn't coming from uneducated people but rather from their well educated minds which are now playing a huge role in the production of so many things that are exported around the globe thus the huge growth in their economy.

How do we fight corruption? How do we win the war against those leaders who misuse their position and their power to achieve their own personal selfish ambitious objectives? How do we gain our human dignity and right to basic life? How do we become part of a peaceful movement that slowly and surely claims back the right to decent life that so many are lacking in our nations and continent? What can each one of us do in order to secure a decent future for our children? Where are we now and where do we want to be? And what do we want from our leaders? These questions often run in my mind, especially when I see another picture or clip of a child dying of starvation in Niger or an innocent civilian being shot dead in Darfur or a middle age man/woman being buried after dying of HIV Aids. Can there be an end to all these man made disasters in our African continent? Yes, there can be an end to these injustices. If you and I act peacefully and strategically - if we let the passion and determination to succeed lead us, then yes I believe one day Africa will be a great developed and prosperous continent. What do we do now? Act! Do the right thing - send your child to school. Struggle today for your child's tomorrow. That's what my parents did and look where it got me - living a much more decent life. Because what's the point for you to suffer extreme poverty today and allow the same to happen to your children tomorrow? Seek, work, encourage and provide for your child's education. Our only hope is to bring up young, bright and knowledgeable future leaders. The only way to reduce corruption and conflicts in our continent is to change people's attitude. If we can plant seeds of honesty and transparency into our young people from an early age, then there is a chance to successfully changing people's attitudes and habits from corruption to honesty.

All educated people in our nation and abroad must rally to support the idea of raising awareness of the importance of education amongst our people. Young and bright students must be mentored and supported financially and practically in order to reach their full potential. Education mustn't only focus on the academic side because not everyone is born academically strong, but the creation of vocational colleges where practical skills are taught is very vital also.

CULTURE, CULTURE, CULTURE

Culture is defined by Cambridge International Dictionary as the way of life or general customs and beliefs of a particular group of people at a particular time.

As a young African woman from Rwanda but born and raised in DR Congo, I am very proud of the culture and heritage that I inherited from both countries. It is not just the riches and joy found in traditional songs, ballads, dance, proverbs, stories, beliefs, musical instruments but it is also the way people greet, mourn or celebrate in different parts of the world that fascinates me. For example, in Rwanda people hug each other when they greet, it is known as "guhoberana" whereas in Congo people just shake hands or in case of young modern Congolese, they kiss three times on the cheeks. In Tanzania, children greet older people by touching them on their head saying "Shikamo" and older people reply "marhaba". The respect given to older people is greater in Africa compared to the West. Socially, people live together and share everything. If you run out of things such as salt, sugar or soap - all you have to do is knock on your next door neighbour and they will give you some. People know everyone's business and are happy to help one another. Like in many other African countries, in Congo and in Rwanda mourning and celebration is very much a community thing. There is no such a thing as private funeral or private marriage. Culturally, there is so much to celebrate and so much to learn from our ancestors, great grandparents, grandparents and parents.

However, many things need changed as well. Some of the practices and traditions do not fit in the 21st century thus the barrier to development. In particular, the gender inequality that exists in most parts of Africa must be addressed and tackled.

The gender inequality that exists in most parts of Africa has been ignored by leaders for many centuries. Women and girls are treated as second class human that are born to be married, give birth, serve and submit to their husbands. Women find it very hard to have equal access to education and work. Yet it is obvious that if a woman is well educated, the children have a better chance of being well educated too. The education of girls and young women must be prioritised as there is more evidence which point to the fact that children who come from families where the mother is educated do well in life. The standard of life is much better where a woman is well educated and professional.

Women must be given a place they deserve. Just as we do appreciate a man's position and their role in the African society so must women be appreciated too. Today more than ever, women are proving that they can not only bring children to the world but can do all that men do, whether it is a physical or mental task. I can not think of any job or post that a man holds and a woman can't. All she needs is equal access to education, training and opportunity. Yet in Africa, millions of women are denied the opportunity to study and develop their intellectual ability. Girls are not encouraged to take active part in the moral, social and political development of their country. In rural areas, young girls are not allowed to attend schools; instead they are trained at home about house work and hard physical work such as farming etc. Countries such as Rwanda where women are being encouraged to contribute and participate in all parts of its development are seeing real results. Despite having been through one of the worst genocides in mankind history, it is one of the few countries in Africa progressing very well.

Sex-education and openness amongst young men and women must be encouraged in order to prevent sexually transmitted diseases. Sex in most parts of Africa is not something you openly talk about. The lack of information in this subject is the cause of transmission of sexually transmitted diseases and early pregnancy. Young people are not adequately informed and are involved in sexual activities at very young age. I was very luck to have parents who openly spoke to us about sex from a young age. They gave us enough information on the consequences of sex at a young age.

One of the cultures that I find very, very hard to accept is the way men are treated or let say treat themselves in most African countries. Most African men have got it in their heads that they marry to be served and women must submit to their decisions at all times. In some parts, even children come after. Also I find it utterly unacceptable that girls and women are encouraged to cope with abusive, unfaithful and often horrible husbands because they have no choice but stay in that marriage.

I can understand when in some cases a woman is trapped in an abusive marriage due to financial reasons because that woman is perhaps afraid to starve her children to death, but generally it seems to be a culture where women must accept everything that is going on and if a woman chooses to separate or divorce for often valid reasons such as unfaithfulness and domestic abuse then she is seen as the bad one and the one at fault. No wonder AIDS is spreading very fast. Many women who discover that their husband have had or are having an affair are not allowed to leave or divorce. If they do, they lose not only their partner but a place in the society.

Whilst it is true that a family unity is wonderful and it is far better to stay in a marriage than divorce, people have to understand that women have rights too. And where one's life is being put at risk by infection of sexually transmitted disease brought in by an unfaithful partner or where one's life is being put through hell by both mental and physical abuse then it is not worth remaining in that marriage. In Africa, the most common reason often given by people trying to keep a woman to a deceiving marriage is "think about the children". Whilst it is true that any separation affect children, people seem to forget that an abusive marriage also affects children in particular psychologically.

As leaders throughout Africa seek to develop the continent, I would encourage them to address the issue surrounding girls' education. Government decision makers must prioritise the education of young girls and must have policies in place which encourage and promote the education of a woman.

SEPARATION

Upon my return home from the hospital, things between Peter and I started to go very wrong. We found ourselves constantly arguing over little things and big things. Whenever I brought up the subject of his unfaithfulness, he would compare it to my relationships before marriage. It infuriated me to see that he could compare the two.

"How dare you compare your unfaithfulness in marriage with my previous relationships? Whatever I did before I met you has nothing to do with our marriage." I would angrily say

Peter seemed to have had it in his head that, because I had boyfriends in the past, it meant the probability of me being unfaithful to him was very high. Like many male Africans, to him virginity meant guarantee of faithfulness in marriage.

Often I would find myself yelling at Peter trying to explain that I never jumped into bed with strangers, and that he had no right to judge me based on my past deeds.

The arguments between Peter and I turned violent with both sides hitting each other. But because he is much stronger than me, I ended up with bruises on my body and reported the beatings to the police. This made the situation worse.

At home in Rwanda, they were worried sick since I had no family in Scotland. Friends were very helpful offering to help with children whenever things got out of hand. In January the Social Work decided to register Nathan and Daniel on the child protection registrar because, sadly, the intensive conflict between Peter and I was affecting them, in particular Nathan who at six was very much aware of what was happening. My world was falling apart in front of me. The perfect golden relationship that I once had with Peter was turning into the worst nightmare of my life. I spent many sleepless nights thinking,

"How can this happen to us? We were the best couple, the unbreakable one. He was the perfect man and I thanked God day and night for giving me such a wonderful husband. Oh God this must be a nightmare and hopefully when I awake the next day, this nightmare won't be there"

I quickly realised that this wasn't a nightmare but a reality. However I wasn't going to give up easily. But as things got worse between Peter and I, friends rallied to support us. My best friend Flora, who lives in England with her husband Robert, phoned to say that they were coming to visit us in order to support and offer us some advice. Peter categorically opposed the visit and made it clear that he didn't want to see them anywhere near our place. I was desperate to talk to somebody from my country and therefore needed my friends to come. They felt the same too and agreed to come and stay in a hotel near us rather than stay with us.

20ᵀᴴ FEBRUARY 2006

Flora and her husband arrived from England in the afternoon and stayed at a local hotel not far from our house. They had come for four days and were hoping to visit us once Peter had calmed down.

"See you later" I said to Peter as I left to go and see my friends.

"Where are you going?" he asked.

"Not far. Just to see some friends and I won't be long."

I was very happy to see my Rwandan friend and her husband. We talked for a long time. Then the police came to the hotel and were looking for me.

"Mrs Mrimi, you have been reported missing" one of the police said

"How did you know I was here?" I asked.

"Your husband guessed that you might be here."

"Well I am safe. Sorry for the trouble."

At home I found Peter extremely angry.

"Where have you been?" he asked, furious.

"I told you that I was going to visit friends."

"What friends?"

"Flora and Robert."

"I told you that I didn't want them to come."

"They had to come. They needed to know how we are. Besides papa and mama asked Flora to come and see if I was alright."

"You don't listen? Do you?" Peter said as he stormed off upstairs to the bedroom.

On their second day, Flora and Robert decided to pay us a visit. As soon as they walked into the house, Peter stormed out of the house without even saying hello to our guests. This time I felt Peter's behaviour had gone too far. It was very bizarre to see that Peter, who had always managed to hide his problems and put on a brave face for the sake of our visitors, could storm off the way he did.

"He'll be fine" I said as I welcomed our guests in to the sitting room.

"I'm sorry if we have caused any trouble" Robert said apologetically.

"It's not your fault, so don't worry, he'll be ok" I said as I tried to put my visitors at ease.

Our friends stayed for a couple of hours.

That night Peter came back very late. I couldn't sleep so I went downstairs to the study.

"You've got some explaining to do" Peter said, as he walked into the study where I was browsing the internet.

"What explaining?"

"Where did you put the money that the bank had loaned us? Why are Flora and Robert here after I repeatedly told you that I didn't want them anywhere near this place? Why don't you listen to me?"

"Peter, we are all adults and we live in a free country. Flora and Robert have the right to go wherever they want. It's not as if they've come to stay in your house. As to the money, we spent it together so don't ask me where the money is!" I calmly replied.

That night, we had the worst argument and ended up fighting. Peter pulled my ears so hard that they started bleeding. I used my strength to get him off me but failed. I ended up spitting on him and started screaming for help.

After realising that I was bleeding, Peter backed off.

"I didn't mean to hurt you" were his words after seeing how bad my ears looked. I pretended to be okay in order to avoid fuelling any further violence.

23ᴿᴰ FEBRUARY 2006

It was time to drop Nathan at school. I prayed and hoped that Peter would drop him alone so that I could stay at home and phone the police. However Peter ordered me to come with him.

"From today, we shall do everything and go everywhere together as a family" he said.

By now I was living with the fear of being beaten again so without arguing we all took Nathan to school. At the school car park, Peter locked me in the car and took Nathan to his class. I managed to open the car door from inside and asked one of the ladies in the car park to look after Daniel while I ran to the nearest shop for help.

The police arrived within minutes and took me to their station where I was interviewed and examined by a doctor. That day Gordon and Mary were planning to take me and my friends Flora and Robert out for lunch. I asked the officer to phone them. Since I wasn't pressing charges the officer promised that I would be able to leave the station by noon. Gordon agreed to collect me at noon.

I was about to leave the station when the officer called me back.

"I'm arresting you for assault......" he said.

"What?" I exclaimed.

"Anything you say ...." he continued.

To say that I was shocked is an understatement.

"How could this happen. I'm the victim here and how come I'm the one being arrested?" I asked in disbelief.

"Your husband is here and has reported that you have assaulted him and is pressing charges" he replied.

"What about my children? Where are they? Are they going to be okay?"

"Your baby is with Karin and Joe. Arrangements have been made for Nathan to join him there."

I was relieved to hear that my children were safe with the family that I had grown to trust very much. Karin and Joe whose son Jos. is Nathan's best friend had been standing with us throughout our problems. They were very supportive, caring and understanding. They were among friends who often took good care of Nathan and Daniel whenever things went very wrong.

"Well if that's case, I'm pressing charges too."

We were both arrested and spent the night in the station's cells. This was yet another nightmare. Spending a freezing night in the police cell was horrible. I was very lucky to be given an extra blanket to stay warm but still felt very cold. I couldn't eat nor drink. After hours of thinking and meditating upon my life, I managed to get about twenty minutes sleep.

The following morning we were both taken to the local Sheriff Court in a reliance van with handcuffs on. I felt like a real criminal - it was such a horrible experience. I was allowed to see my solicitor who promised to do her best.

After hours of waiting for the hearing, an officer walked into the court cell where I was waiting.

"Mrs Mrimi, you are free to go" he said.

"What happened? I asked looking quite surprised to hear that I was being freed without even being called to the court.

"The case has been cancelled because there are no witnesses. Since it's your word against your husband's, the sheriff can't decide on your case and has decided to let you go."

"Well, thanks" I said, relieved to finally leave the place where I was locked up like a criminal.

After what seemed to be like a decade in the cells I was free at last.

That night, I had been doing a lot of serious thinking about my future. I spent the whole night thinking:

"Do I really want to go back to a relationship that is not working? I'm sick and tired of the endless fighting. After the confessions, I don't even love and trust Peter anymore. I was ready to forgive him and give him a second chance. However my efforts and attempts have been ruined by constant arguments and beatings. What about my children? Will they be okay without me? I'm not very helpful to them right now due to my illness so I

suppose they will be fine. Will I manage to live without seeing them every day? What if Peter takes them away from me? Where will I go? Am I safe out there without Peter and my children? Will I really cope on my own? How will friends and family react when they hear about the separation?

I knew my marriage was collapsing and I didn't have much feeling left for Peter. However the thought of leaving him petrified me. I wasn't confident enough to face life on my own. I was brought up in a society where women depended on their husbands not only for financial means but for emotional and moral support. I grew up thinking that life without a husband is meaningless.

I spent the whole night weighing the advantages and disadvantages of leaving my dear husband. After such an intense battle of thoughts within me, I decided it was safer and better for me not to go back home. I went to my friend Sandra and spent the afternoon with her. Having witnessed the struggles of my relationship, she too advised me to take a break.

HOMELESS

At on of the Glenrothes local offices, the receptionist advised me that it was too late to help and gave me a twenty four hours emergency number for homeless people. With no mobile or money for a payphone I headed to the nearest police station. The receptionist explained that they didn't deal with my kind of problems. I was desperate so I decided to make myself comfortable and fell asleep in the waiting room.

"Mrs Mrimi?" a voice called.

"Yes" I replied, waking up from my deep sleep.

"We have contacted the homeless office and they have agreed to arrange something for you. Someone will contact you very soon."

"Thank you very much" I said, surprised to see that the receptionist had changed her mind and got in-touch with the homeless team.

It wasn't long before someone from the homeless office phoned back to confirm that they'd booked a hotel for me in Rosyth.

"How will I get there?" I asked.

"Do you have anyone who can take you?"

"No."

"Have you got any money for taxi?"

"No."

"Okay, I will arrange for a taxi to collect you as soon as possible" she kindly said.

At the hotel I lay down in my bed thinking *"what have I done?"*

I could not sleep but thought of my children whom I hadn't seen for a couple of days.

The following day I was moved from the hotel to a homeless hostel in Buckhaven. I had, prior to my move there, heard how infamous the place was due to its reputation of housing people on drugs. As I walked in to the hostel I could not help but wonder if I was doing the right thing. *"How could I leave my beautiful home in exchange for this place? Will I survive this place if there are a lot of drug addicts in here?"*

After signing the agreements and completing many forms, I was shown my room. The hostel was a huge manse. It had just been decorated and refurbished. It looked better and cleaner so the first impression that I got from the place was good. I got to meet staff and residents. Everyone was very nice including those whom I suspected were probably on drugs. Most residents quickly became my good friends. We shared our ups and downs which helped very much. When you are going through hardship you tend to think you are the only one hurting until you speak to others and quickly realise you are not the only one. Most nights we met in the sitting room and would chat for hours. I often shared my African experience and my poor background with my new found friends. Residents couldn't understand me when I told them that to me the hostel was like Buckingham Palace.

"What? You call this place Buckingham Palace?" one of them exclaimed.

"Of course I do. You can't have lived in a hut and not look at this place as a palace."

People are very much blessed in this country. It's amazing to see how people's basic rights are met by the government. From education to social and health care, services provided are almost perfect - well compared to where I come from. The value put upon a human being in this country is probably a million times more than the value that a human being in Africa gets. In most parts of Africa, you have to be rich and famous in order to receive half the attention and care that a normal person receives in Britain.

LEGAL BATTLE

I got in touch with Social Work to organise contact with my sons. I wanted to have them with me but I wasn't in the position to do so due to my mental illness. Contact with the boys had to be supervised. At one point I was considered a danger to my children because during my illness the baby had accidentally fallen down the stairs. I had asked Nathan to keep an eye on his brother whom I had placed on the stairs in order to go to the kitchen to get something. That day, Peter had been thrown out due to a heated argument that I had with him. Suddenly I heard a bang and the baby screamed. I rushed to the stairs only to find Daniel at the bottom. Luckily he'd been placed only three to four steps from the bottom so he wasn't injured. This incident, combined with the one near Glasgow's M8 with Nathan, made professionals decide that I was not a fit mother. If there is anything that hurts mothers most; it's when you are perceived as an unfit mother and your children are taken away from you. Although my sons weren't physically taken away from me, the fact that I wasn't allowed to be with them, when I had left their father felt, almost the same as someone taking them away from me. I needed the all clear from the psychiatrist consultant before I could get unsupervised contact with my children, never mind their custody of them.

Even though I had returned to work after my hell of maternity leave and was coping quite well, I still needed psychiatric assistance. I was being seen by the consultant and community psychiatric nurse every month. I was also kept on anti-psychosis medication.

Some professionals, who knew how ill I was, thought it was going to be a long time before I would be given custody of my children. I refused to remain ill and embarked on a journey to complete healing. My number one priority was to get well and be with my children. I had never felt so lonely in my life. Without them and without my family, it was as if life had no meaning anymore. Sometimes I could feel the pain physically and a night never passed by without me crying. I missed the baby very much because babies grow fast. Nathan's noise, questioning and cheekiness suddenly became distant. During this dark episode of my life's journey, I tried to pen my feelings and they included the following:

05TH APRIL 2006

Oh God, today seems to be very hard. I feel so low and feel like crying! Why? I don't know. Life is so hard without my precious little boys. I miss Peter too and I just wish things didn't turn out this way. Such a happy family, such a happy beginning, such a respected couple with so many positive things going on for them (good jobs, nice house, good cars, two gorgeous children, strong faith in God, intimate relationship, understanding and care, education etc) and now all gone. What is left is like a hole in my life which will take a long time to fill. I don't know how and when this huge hole will be filled but I know it will. Things may seem horrible now but I'm determined to live my life to the full and shall not allow loneliness, depression, fear and uncertainty to spoil it. Friends have been very helpful and my faith in God keeps me going. Nathan and Daniel are the reason why I'm still around and let's hope that I get to see them more often and without restrictions and supervision.

Thank you, Jesus, for being the pillar and tower of my life, I'm glad that I have you to run to when there is no one around. Your presence fills me with the sense of belonging and security. Where I have been rejected by the person I most loved and trusted, you are there, so please help me carry on this difficult journey of life.

All honour, power and praise belong to you alone now and forevermore, amen.

22ND APRIL 2006

In the presence of God I find my refuge when my world falls apart. In you, oh Lord, I find peace and assurance that justice will be done one day. In this world, we come and go. All that we achieve is good but just like us, they do pass away and everything will disappear onc day, but you oh Lord live for eternity. Your love endures forever. Your mercy and grace are new each morning. You set our lives before us, you determine our ways and call us to obey your commandments without which, this world would be in a terrible mess. When others do not understand me, when I'm let down by not only the people around me, but the government systems upon which I put my trust for a fair and just judgement, then Lord thank you that I can confidently come to you and receive that fairness and justice that people around me can not give me. Dear Lord, I am weak, confused and tired. I'm in a very serious need for your guidance, wisdom and love. Holy one, I can no longer go on like this, what do I do? How do I make my decisions? I am thirty and once thought that I was very mature to deal and cope with anything that would come my way but how wrong I was? Because now, I don't seem to be coping well with what has happened to my family. It feels as if all that I had, has gone with the relationship that I had with Peter. My confidence, myself, everything feels empty. Maybe I feel empty because I don't have my children with me but then there are people who don't have children, so why should I not learn to just get on with it. Please Lord help me, please do.

The whole thing is very painful and very hurting, my emotions are all over the place this morning and the only way is to talk to someone that I trust with all my heart, and that is you, my Lord Jesus, because you came to this world and suffered for me even though you are eternally holy. You left your glory and divine kingdom to come and rescue me, not only from the sins that take people to eternal hell but also from the fear and uncertainty that tend to destabilise us in our journey of life. Holy and loving father God, please tend me now as I feel lonely, angry, disappointed and defeated by the current circumstances of my life. I really need you to be closer to me now more than ever, because it is scary, and the judgement of what is best for me now would be affected by these tides and strong waves so please step in and help me in whatever decision I make that it would be sound and pleasing to you.

8TH MAY 2006

I hate myself because I'm a failure and my life is a mess. I don't like myself anymore and I feel let down by life. God, where are you? I need you very much, please let me see you and hear you loud and clear. Where do I go and what do I do? How do I overcome such a hard battle in my life? My mind is filled with negative thoughts even though I know that I have so much to be grateful for. There are many good things in my life but where are they now that I most need them? Financially I'm seriously broke and emotionally I cannot take it any longer.

I despair Lord because I don't see the end of the tunnel. Please help me I pray, please come. Come Lord Jesus, please come. I will not take any silly decision because this is just a dark chapter in the book of my life that I'm going through. Hopefully the end of this dark chapter is near and the beginning of a better one is starting soon. All I need from you Lord is the strength to carry on, the will to live and the hope to overcome. I wish things were different but you alone, oh Lord, know why you have allowed this to happen. There must be a purpose for this battle but the problem is I'm not strong enough to carry on fighting. I'm extremely tired and am in great need of your help. I'm fed up and I am really tired. I honestly don't know how I could carry on like this. Lord you need to do something about my inner suffering. The pain, the financial worries and uncertainty of the court outcome have all taken their toll on me and I feel battered. Maybe I'm paying for something that I did in the past or maybe it is just life. I don't know what to think anymore and I don't know how to keep positive. Whatever is happening to me Lord, please help, and please do so now or else I go under.

8TH MAY 2006

Dear Father God

I'm sick and tired of this life! When is it going to end? I'm emotionally tired. Do I deserve this? Maybe! Even if I do deserve it, Lord please have mercy, I'm begging you to help me Father. I'm very tired and I'm really,

really fed up. I don't know what to do, please help! Let my cry for help reach you and please act now because I'm tired. I don't know what to think anymore. Sometimes, I don't even know who I am anymore. I feel a total failure and my present life feels horrible. I hate everything. The people I love most are not physically close to me. I miss my children so much and I miss my family too. Dear heavenly Father, why are you not taking me in your heavenly home? I think I will be safe and free of problems there, so please take me.

Nathan and Daniel, I love you with all my heart. I promise to always be there for you. Wherever I go, I shall be with you always. I will never leave you alone for you are my precious, gorgeous little boys, given to me by God Almighty. You are my reason for life and whenever I think of you I praise God for he has given me the perfect children whom I deeply love and care for. In my lowest point, I just have to think of you and the light shines, a smile comes on my face and the future looks bright. You are my hope and my destiny. My Lord is good. Thank you, Lord, for giving me Nathan and Daniel. Even though my prayer is to go in your heavenly home now, my wish is to first take good care of my children, so please provide me with the strength to carry on.

15 MAY 2006

I can do it. I'm more than capable and I'm willing to succeed. I'm absolutely determined to do well if not for me but for my children and others. I'm not meant to fail but succeed. So far I have done very well. Despite the daily emotional struggle, I believe that I'm getting there. This year has been very hard. A marriage breakdown is the worst thing that can happen to anyone. It's so hard to understand how two people who once thought they were one in everything could go their own ways just like that! Yet I'm very positive that, no matter how hard life may seem now there is light at the end of the dark tunnel, there is hope in Jesus and there is a bright future.

"You've done so well." one of my friends said recently. "People didn't think you could do it but you have proved them wrong."

SUPERVISED VISITS

Social work organised and supervised the contacts between my children and myself. I saw them twice a week and each contact lasted about an hour. It was extremely difficult to see my children for a very short time and without the freedom of doing things with them. Peter was not speaking to me and I found it very hard to deal with him.

Prior to our separation we had planned going home to Africa for the Easter holidays. The situation had since changed and I wasn't in the position to travel with Peter so I opted out of the trip. He decided to go ahead with the trip taking our two children with him. After all the pain and heartache between us, I strongly felt there was a possibility that he wouldn't bring them back. I spoke to my lawyer and we took the case to court for an interdict.

The hearing took place on the day before Peter and the children were due to leave. I was very relieved to hear that the sheriff had ordered Peter not take the children with him. However this verdict fuelled anger and bitterness in Peter - as a result he stopped all the contact that I was having with Nathan and Daniel. Since these arrangements were amicable and informal, there was nothing Social Work could do. I felt hopeless and helpless. Luckily my solicitor managed to get the case looked at quickly by the sheriff. But a couple of weeks passed by without seeing my children. During this period I managed to see Nathan at school during his lunch break.

After days of struggle and pain, the sheriff agreed for me to see the boys for four hours every Saturday and Sunday. The contact had to be supervised by friends. It was my worst nightmare to have to leave my children after each visit. However the hope that I would one day be given their custody kept me going. I needed to be strong and fight my case. I tried to stay positive even though it was very hard. Friends were magnificent. Some took me out for meals; some took me to yoga classes etc. My minister and his family supported me very much. I honestly don't know where I would be today without the support from my minister and his family. The support and help that I received from the Doyle family go beyond my imagination. To this day, they remain my closest friends. Without a doubt they are like my family. Only God knows how grateful I am to them. Members of my church were very supportive too. They prayed for me and always asked after me.

I filed for custody. On the first hearing, the court decided to appoint a lawyer in order to investigate the case and make recommendations. This was my chance to prove that I was perfectly capable of looking after my children. My solicitor advised me to look for a flat or house in order to increase my chances of gaining custody. Luckily I was back at work and was in the financial position to pay for rented accommodation. After an extensive search, I finally moved and settled into a beautiful ground floor flat with two bedrooms. Friends donated lot of stuff and within a few weeks I had a beautiful home.

The court case was scheduled for 14th June. Mr Glass who was investigating the case interviewed both Peter and I. Friends who knew us well were also interviewed. Mentally, I had made a good recovery and my doctor had been very positive about my case. When I saw the doctor again for the court report, he was confident that I was mentally fit to be the main carer of my children.

14TH JUNE 2006

At the court, my lawyer showed me a long report that had been prepared by Mr Glass.

"I want to show you the best part of this report" she said.

She went straight to the recommendations which were most likely to be adopted by the sheriff. The court reporter recommended that I become the main carer of the children.

"Oh my God, I can't believe it" I exclaimed, since I wasn't expecting this to happen so soon.

I was shaking with joy and couldn't believe that I might finally be allowed to be a mother after four months of being denied just that.

I knew Nathan who was old enough to understand things would be over the moon too. He'd at each of my contact with him said how he wanted to be with me forever.

Peter, whom I expected to disagree with these recommendations, seemed to have lost the motivation for more fights.

Shortly before the calling of our case, his lawyer approached mine to explain that Peter had agreed to hand over the children without any problems. Peter's co-operation was a real victory because I didn't want the legal battle to carry on. The children would go to stay with him every weekend.

Peter needed time to pack their belongings so we agreed that he would drop them off the following day at my minister's house.

I came back to work and as usual I immediately wrote my feelings of joy:

I can't even begin to express my joy about today's court outcome. Thank you, God, for allowing justice to happen. I'm overjoyed at the fact that my precious children Nathan and Daniel are now allowed to reside with me. This is the light at the end of a very dark tunnel. I love them to bits and I live for them. Everything I do is for them and my sole purpose on this earth is to serve and take care of them. I live to worship God too and without His Majesty none of this would have happened. God has used many people to bring justice. The Sheriff, Mr Glass, Dr Dickson, Dr Michael, Gordon, Mary, Sophie, Lynn, John and Diane etc have all been a great help. I'm ecstatic and very pleased.

However that night I couldn't sleep thinking the worst. *"What if Peter decides to run away with them? What if something dreadful happens to them? He seemed to have changed his tone and attitude, is everything okay? Or has he planned to take the children away with him?"*

Luckily, Peter brought the children and some of their belongings as agreed. That night we stayed with Gordon, Mary and Sophie celebrating my reunion with my sons. I was very happy to be with my boys again and Nathan was very excited too.

"Mum I will now have two homes like my best friend Oliver. He stays with his mum but goes to his dad on weekends" he said.

"Yes darling, that's right" I replied.

Nathan had coped very well during the turmoil of my relationship with his father. He's a very wise and sensible boy. Even though the separation had hit him badly, he seemed to think that it was quite normal for mothers and fathers to stay apart. Some of his friends were in exactly the same situation. I don't think it would have been the same if this had happened to us in Africa where it's still quite unusual to see a couple separating. In Africa, separation is seen as a disgrace and as a result, children suffer most when a couple separate. Having said that, things are fast changing in Africa particularly in big cities where women are quickly becoming more empowered and independent.

EPILOGUE

Although life as a single parent is hard indeed, my sons and I are now living very happily together. The boys see their father as much as possible and I have managed to hold on to my job, write and look after my precious boys at the same time. I'm determined more than ever to provide Nathan and Daniel with the best and loving environment. I don't regret marrying Peter because he'd given me the best six years of our marriage and gave me two beautiful children. He was once a nice, gentle and patient husband. It's very unfortunate that our marriage ended in disaster. I wish him all the best and it's my hope that he will remain a committed father to Nathan and Daniel, who love him very much.

Nathan is now in primary three and is doing very well. His favourite subjects include Maths and Reading. His brother Daniel is now eleven months and has been walking since he was about ten months. He has recently learned the game of throwing everything in the toilet. A few days ago, Nathan left his half apple on the table in order to attend to something; Daniel took the apple and headed towards the toilet. I was just about to stop him when he let go the apple and there it was in the toilet. I had to do the unpleasant job of getting it out of the toilet as it wouldn't flush. He then looked at me with a cheeky face as if to say *"who is clever, huh?"*

I am thankful to see that Nathan and Daniel have a better start in life than me. It is my prayer that children currently living in extreme poverty across the world would work hard today and receive financial and practical support from us all so that in the future, they will grow into adults who will provide a better life for their children. When I look back at my childhood and I look at my children's life, I am amazed at the difference between the two lives - mine as a child and theirs. Where I didn't know if I will eat at all, my children have a huge variety of food to choose from. I am thankful to God for helping me throughout my life, thankful to Scotland/Britain - a nation that has taken care of me, given me an education and a place to live, thankful to my sponsor who made it possible for me to come here and thankful to all who have played a part in making my life better.

Back in Rwanda, my parents live a much better life compared to what they had in DR Congo. They live in a four bedroom house in the outskirts of the capital city of Kigali. Papa has recently retired from his job as the head of Personnel at the Institute of Agriculture and Husbandry. However, soon after his retirement he was called back to work on a temporary basis. I suppose the Institute was finding it difficult to fill the vacancy with an experienced person like papa. To this day, Papa is still my rock and star. His courage, optimism and determination for his children's success have transformed our lives for better and for ever. He worked very hard, waking up early in the morning to cultivate the land before changing his clothes in order to go to his work so that we didn't starve. He gave us the much needed guidance and his strictness meant bringing up children who respected and valued others.

As usual, mama is a house wife dedicated to serving her husband and family. She is a very patient woman who has tirelessly worked hard to give us the best. She filled us with love, care and affection. Without her dedication, endurance and optimism, none of us would have made it to where we are. She constantly made us feel valued even when we had nothing to make us feel valued.

My brother Emmanuel graduated in 2004 with a Bachelor of Science in Computer science and is currently working for the Ministry of Education in Rwanda. Soon after his graduation, Emmanuel married Brigitte and they have a beautiful daughter called Deborah who is just a month younger than Daniel.

Annie and Marie are currently doing secretarial studies and hope to complete the course next year. Louis is in boarding school where he is still studying for his secondary education. Charlotte our youngest sister has nearly completed her primary education. She used to be the black sheep of the family because she was spoilt very much as she was the last born. However she has grown into a beautiful, calm and serious girl who doesn't misbehave anymore.

Rwanda as a country has come a long way. Security in the country has improved very much. Given what had happened to the country in 1994, you would think Rwanda would be far behind compared to other African nations in terms of economic and technology development but it is actually one of the few African's countries to be developing very fast. The record number of graduates in Rwanda has risen sharply with more people opting to do a Masters Degree.

The country's institute of science and technology is renowned in the central and east African regions. Rwandans across the world have invested not only their money in the country but their time and wealth of experience gained from other countries. Despite many difficulties which include the pain, hurt and bitterness caused by the genocide, the work of reconciliation and justice is bearing tangible results such as tolerance and forgiveness between the two tribes. I take this opportunity to commend and congratulate the president of Rwanda Mr. Paul Kagame and his team who tirelessly promote the unity, justice and fairness in our beloved nation of Rwanda.

I give thanks day and night to God Almighty who, through Jesus Christ and the Holy Spirit, strengthens me day by day. I am a living testimony that there is a God and He does passionately love us in particular when we are going through trials in our lives. I would be lost and dead if it wasn't for my faith in God. May the same God, whose miracles I have lived to witness and have seen all my life, bless you abundantly as a result of reading this book.

AMBITIONS

I often look back at my life and think "Wow! What a great and fabulous life I have had!" It has not been perfect especially with the disastrous ending of my marriage to Peter. However there's been more to my life to be grateful for than to be miserable about. I strongly believe that to have come from such extreme poverty to where I am is not by chance but by purpose. There must be a reason why God has allowed me to be where I am. The purpose is the passion which burns in my heart everyday. The passion is to join campaigners of the make poverty history. I want to be part of a movement that will make a positive impact to an African child. I want to join a group that campaigns on the need to educate young Africans. I want to be involved in the on-going development of the African continent by joining hands with fellow human beings across the globe whose aim is to campaign against the extreme poverty reigning in most parts of Africa. I try to be realistic and tell myself that the development of the African continent will not happen overnight. At the same time I visualise a future that could be very bright and prosperous for Africa. The only way to secure such a future is to educate young Africans. I do have hope in some of our African leaders. But I do despair when I see how mismanagement of funds and corruption are destroying our continent. Yet there is hope for Africa. One of the topics I wrote about during my illness was the education of African children. I wrote this topic from a personal point of view. I know for sure that none of my achievements would have happened without education. I am currently acting as my organisation's manager and I can't help but think *"how on earth could I have been in this position had it not been for the education that I received?"* Not only does my work pay me enough money to have a comfortable life for myself and my children but the salary also enables me to help my parents and family have a better and comfortable life. Without education and literacy, my chances of success would have been non-existent.

The literacy rate in Africa is very low compared other continents. The lowest literacy rate is in Niger where only thirteen percent of adults are literate. South Africa, Seychelles and Zimbabwe have the highest rates where eighty three to eighty five percent of their adult population are literate[5].

Literacy is an essential key to any society's development. I do hope that there will be more campaigns to raise awareness on the importance of the education of all African children in particular in countries such as Niger and Sudan where the literacy rate is very low. I wish African governments could quickly come up with ideas on how to tackle illiteracy. The best ideas must be implemented. This could be the best solution to ending the civil wars and tribal conflicts in our continent because as I said earlier in my education topic, it is very easy to corrupt and brainwash an illiterate mind whereas it is hard to do the same to a well informed mind. We don't need research or evidence to prove that countries where literacy is high seem to be developed and peaceful.

With the help and commitment of people living abroad, I think the African Diaspora can play a huge role in promoting the education and welfare of African children. Below is something to think about.

One Africa, one people

"God can only work with people in order to help, comfort and prosper the weak, poor, sick and helpless victims of this world's on-going wars and injustice"

The gap between developed and developing countries is obvious. This gap instead of narrowing continues to expand due to many facts which include the fact that developed countries heavily invest in their people i.e. the provision of basic life requirements such as food, shelter, health, education, security etc whereas most developing countries mainly in Africa invest in weapons, wars, corruption, hate , tribalism etc.

Of course there are many other factors that affect the development of most Africans countries. But these factors are complex issues which require long-term solutions by powerful states and should not be prioritised now as lives are at stake. It's time for Africans to stop blaming others and pointing the finger at other factors such as colonisation, trade rules, conditional aid etc. It's also time we stopped waiting on others, namely the West and America, to come and solve our problems. We Africans must take matters into our own hands and start doing something about our wars, famine, diseases, lack of education etc. While situations in Africa may seem enormous to challenge and very complex to even try to find solutions, we can only work together in a positive way towards the goal of building the continent rather than destroying it. It's you, and I, who live in countries where freedom of speech exists, who will voice concerns on behalf of our fellow Africans who are voiceless. We must work together to do something. We have been watching silently for too long. Now is the time to act and do what we can to help. Whatever assistance we can bring to our people is far better than doing nothing.

It is apparent and obvious that most disasters in Africa such as wars, famine, unnecessary deaths caused by preventable diseases etc are not only man-made but are also preventable. But who will prevent these horrible circumstances from taking Africans' lives unnecessarily? The prevention will not always come from the West and North America nor will it come from Australia and Japan not even from heaven if we do not work together as Africans to positively impact and save lives. We have been divided for a very long time. Now is the time to unite and act.

The immediate international aid and intervention is greatly appreciated and will be needed until Africa is mature enough to sustain itself. Genuine people like as Bob Geldof, Bill Gates, Bono and their teams, together with many un-named individuals, have been very supportive and are spending their time, money and resources to help feed and educate the poor. I am very grateful for their work and the on-going work of Aids agencies such as Red Cross, Oxfam, World Vision, Christian Aid etc, because frankly without them, God knows how many more millions of lives would have perished. Even individuals who donate a pound or a dollar are making a huge difference in the world of extreme poverty. There are many other projects and initiatives which have been started by Africans in Africa to solve some of these problems both in the short-term and long term. Positive steps have been taken by well governed countries to further develop people and technology. There are so many good things happening in Africa right now which must be acknowledged, but unfortunately these may not mean a lot when a neighbour or fellow national is starving to death in an era where man is landing in space.

Africans living abroad must join hands to ensure that the education of young Africans is provided free of charge and if it means rich people subsidising for poor people so be it.

My prayer and hope is that the African Diaspora living in Scotland and in the United Kingdom will soon come together in order to have an open discussion on the role that the African Diaspora living here can play in promoting the education of our children back home.

I am in search of people who would like me to join them in this kind of campaign. I am also in search of people who would like to join me in this campaign.

I have a second project in mind which is about conducting research on whether making poverty history in Africa is a realistic vision and if so how can it be achieved. If you are interested in this project please contact me using the e-mail below.

If you are interested in any of my ideas, I would encourage you to get in-touch with me at cmrimi@yahoo.co.uk I welcome your suggestions and ideas on how to move forward with the **"Educating Every African Child"** campaign which is part of what I want to do in the future.

(FOOTNOTES)

[1] Origin: Britannica Concise Encyclopaedia.

[2] Dowry price is a traditional price given to the bride's family by the groom's family. In Rwanda, the price relates to cows.

[3] HNC: High National certificate.

[4] MP: Member of Parliament

[5] Source: http://www.overpopulation.com/faq/health/education/literacy/africa.html